I0626116

THE 13 STEPS TO RICHES

BASED ON THE WORK BY NAPOLEON HILL IN THINK AND GROW RICH

CREATED BY MULTI #1 INTERNATIONAL BESTSELLING AUTHOR & AWARD WINNING SPEAKER ON HABITS

ERIK SWANSON

THE
13 STEPS TO
RICHES

Featuring
Erik Swanson & Kevin Harrington

#1 BESTSELLER

SIXTH SENSE
HABITUDE
VOLUME 13
WARRIOR

Foreword by Cheri Tree

Copyright © 2024
THE 13 STEPS TO RICHES

All rights reserved. No part of this publication may be reproduced, distributed, or transmitted in any form or by any means, including photocopying, recording, or other electronic or mechanical methods, without the prior written permission of the publishers and Habitude Warrior Int., except in the case of brief quotations embodied in critical reviews and certain other noncommercial uses permitted by copyright law. For permission requests, write to the publishers, addressed "Attention: Permissions Coordinators," at *Team@integritypub.com.*

Permission was granted and approved to use Celebrity Author's testimonials and contributing chapters, quotes, and thoughts throughout the book series, but it is understood that each contributing author and celebrity author are their own entities, and Habitude Warrior International is not responsible or endorse any opinions or actions thereby taken by said authors. Quantity sales special discounts are available on quantity purchases by corporations, associations, and others. For details, contact the publisher at the address above.

Orders by U.S. trade bookstores and wholesalers.

Email: *Team@IntegrityPub.com*

Manufactured and printed in the United States of America and distributed globally by Beyond Publishing and Integrity Publishing.

Hardback ISBN: 978-1-964330-17-4
Paperback ISBN: 978-1-964330-16-7

TESTIMONIALS
THE 13 STEPS TO RICHES

"What an honor to collaborate with so many personal development leaders from around the world as we Co-Author together honoring the amazing principles by Napoleon Hill in this new book series, *The 13 Steps to Riches*, by Habitude Warrior and Erik "Mr. Awesome" Swanson. Well done, "Mr. Awesome," for putting together such an amazing series. If you want to up-level your life, read every book in this series and learn to apply each of these time-tested steps and principles."

Denis Waitley ~ Author of *Psychology of Winning & The NEW Psychology of Winning—Top Qualities of a 21st Century Winner*

"Just as *Think and Grow Rich* reveals the 13 steps to success discovered by Napoleon Hill after interviewing the richest people around the world (and many who considered themselves failures) in the early 1900s, *The 13 Steps to Riche*s, produced by Habitude Warrior and Erik Swanson takes a modern look at those same 13 steps. It brings together many of today's personal development leaders to share their stories of how *The 13 Steps to Riches* have created and propelled their own successes. I am honored to participate and share the power of Faith in my life. If you truly want to accelerate reaching the success you deserve, read every volume of *The 13 Steps to Riches*."

Sharon Lechter ~ 5-Time N.Y. Times Bestselling Author. Author of *Think and Grow Rich for Women*, Co-Author of *Exit Rich, Rich Dad Poor Dad, Three Feet from Gold, Outwitting the Devil* and *Success and Something Greater*

"The most successful book on personal achievement ever written is now being elaborated upon by many of the world's top thought leaders. I'm honored to Co-Author this series on the amazing principles from Napoleon Hill, in *The 13 Steps to Riches*, by Habitude Warrior, Erik "Mr. Awesome" Swanson."

Jim Cathcart ~ Bestselling Author of *Relationship Selling* and *The Acorn Principle*, among many others. Certified Speaking Professional (CSP) and Former President of the National Speakers Association (NSA)

"Some books are written to be read and placed on the shelf. Others are written to transform the reader, as they travel down a path of true transcendence and enlightenment. *The 13 Steps to Riches* by Habitude Warrior and Erik Swanson is the latter. Profoundly insightful, it revitalizes the techniques and strategies written by Napoleon Hill by applying a modern perspective, and a fearsome collaboration of some of the greatest minds and thought leaders from around the globe. A must-read for all of those who seek to break free of their current levels of success, and truly extract the greatness that lies within. It is an honor and a privilege to have been selected to participate, in what is destined to be the next historic chapter in the meteoric rise of many men and women around the world."

Glenn Lundy ~ Husband to one, Father to 8, Automotive Industry Expert, Author of *The Morning 5*, Creator of the popular morning show #riseandgrind and the Founder of "Breakfast With Champions"

"How exciting to team up with the amazing Habitude Warrior community of leaders such as Erik Swanson, Sharon Lechter, John Assaraf, Denis Waitley and so many more transformational and self-help icons to bring you these timeless and proven concepts in the fields of success and wealth. *The 13 Steps to Riches* book series will help you reach your dreams and accomplish your goals faster than you have ever experienced before!"

Dame Marie Diamond ~ Featured in *The Secret*, Modern-Day Spiritual Teacher, Inspirational Speaker, Feng Shui Master

"If you are looking to crystalize your mightiest dream, rekindle your passion, break through limiting beliefs, and learn from those who have done exactly what you want to do—read this book! In this transformational masterpiece, *The 13 Steps to Riches*, self-development guru Erik Swanson has collected the sage wisdom and time-tested truths from subject matter experts and amalgamated them into a one-stop-shop resource library that will change your life forever!"

Dan Clark ~ Speaker Hall of Fame & N.Y. Times Bestselling Author of *The Art of Significance*

"Life has always been about who you surround yourself with. I am in excellent company with this collaboration from my fellow authors and friends, paying tribute to the life-changing principles by Napoleon Hill in this amazing new book series, *The 13 Steps to Riches*, organized by Habitude Warrior's founder and my dear friend, Erik Swanson. Hill said, 'Your big opportunity may be right where you are now.' This book series is a must-read for anyone who wants to change their lives and prosper, starting now."

Alec Stern ~ America's Startup Success Expert, Co-Founder of Constant Contact

"Finally, a book series that encompasses the lessons the world needs to learn and apply, but in our modern day era. As I always teach my students to "Say YES, and then figure out how," I strongly urge you to do the same. Say YES to adding all of these 13 books in *The 13 Steps to Riches* book series into your success library and watch both your business as well as your personal life grow as a result."

Loral Langemeier ~ 5 Time N.Y. Times Bestselling Author, Featured in *The Secret*, Author of *The Millionaire Maker,* and *YES! Energy - The Equation to Do Less, Make More*

"Napoleon Hill had a tremendous impact on my consciousness when I was very young—there were very few books nor the type of trainings that we see today to lead us to success. Whenever you have the opportunity to read and harness *The 13 Steps to Riches* as they are presented in this series, be happy (and thankful) that there were many of us out there applying the principles, testing the teachings, making the mistakes, and now being offered to you in a way that they are clear, simple and concise—with samples and distinctions that will make it easier for you to design a successful life which includes adding value to others, solving world problems, and making the world work for 100% of humanity... Read on... those dreams are about to come true!"

> *Dame Doria Cordova* ~ CEO of Money & You, Excellerated Business School, Global Business Developer, Ambassador of New Education

"Success leaves clues, and the Co-Authors in this awesome book series, *The 13 Steps to Riches*, will continue the Napoleon Hill legacy with tools, tips, and modern-day principles that greatly expand on the original masterpiece... *Think and Grow Rich*. If you are serious about living your life to the max, get this book series now!"

> *John Assaraf* ~ Chairman & CEO NeuroGym, MrNeuroGym.com, N.Y. Times Bestselling author of *Having It All*, *Innercise*, and *The Answer*. Also featured in *The Secret*

"Over the years, I have been blessed with many rare and amazing opportunities to invest my time and energy. These opportunities require a keen eye and immediate action. This is one of those amazing opportunities for you as a reader! I highly recommend you pick up every book in this series of *The 13 Steps to Riches* by Habitude Warrior and Erik Swanson! Learn from modern-day leaders who have embraced the lessons from the great Napoleon Hill in his classic book from 1937, *Think and Grow Rich*."

Kevin Harrington ~ Original "Shark" on Shark Tank, Creator of the Infomercial, Pioneer of the 'As Seen on TV' brand, Co-Author of *Mentor to Millions*

"When you begin your journey, you will quickly learn of the importance of the first step of *The 13 Steps to Riches*. A burning desire is the start of all worthwhile achievements. Erik 'Mr. Awesome' Swanson's newest book series contains a wealth of assistance to make your journey both successful and enjoyable. Start today... because tomorrow is not guaranteed on your calendar."

Don Green ~ 45 Years of Banking, Finance & Entrepreneurship, Bestselling Author of *Everything I Know About Success I Learned From Napoleon Hill* & *Napoleon Hill My Mentor: Timeless Principles to Take Your Success to the Next Level* & *Your Millionaire Mindset*

Our minds become magnetized with the dominating thoughts we hold in our minds and these magnets attract to us the forces, the people, the circumstances of life which harmonize with the nature of our dominating thoughts.

(Napoleon Hill)

Global Speakers Mastermind & Habitude Warrior Masterminds

Join us and become a member of our tribe! Our Global Speakers Mastermind is a virtual group of amazing thinkers and leaders who meet twice a month. Sessions are designed to be 'to the point' and focused while sharing fantastic techniques to grow your mindset as well as your pocketbooks. We also include famous guest speaker spots for our private Masterclasses. We also designate certain sessions for our members to mastermind with each other & and counsel on the topics discussed in our previous Masterclasses. It's time for you to join a tribe who truly cares about **YOU** and your future and start surrounding yourself with the famous leaders and mentors of our time. It is time for you to up-level your life, businesses, and relationships.

For more information to check out our Masterminds:
Team@HabitudeWarrior.com
www.DecideTobeAwesome.com

BECOME AN INTERNATIONAL
#1 BESTSELLING AUTHOR & SPEAKER

Habitude Warrior International has been highlighting award-winning Speakers and #1 Bestselling Authors for over 25 years. They know what it takes to become #1 in your field and how to get the best exposure around the world. If you have ever considered giving yourself the GIFT of becoming a well-known Speaker and a fantastically well known #1 Best-Selling Author, then you should email their team right away to find out more information in how you can become involved. They have the best of the best when it comes to resources in achieving the bestselling status in your particular field. Start surrounding yourself with the N.Y. Times Bestsellers of our time and start seeing your dreams become reality!

For more information to become a #1 Bestselling Author & Speaker on our Habitude Warrior Conferences Please text the word AUTHORS to 619-304-6268 And also go to: www.DecideToBeAwesome.com

Acknowledgement To Napoleon Hill

I would like to personally acknowledge and thank the one and only Napoleon Hill for his work, dedication, and, most importantly, his belief in himself. Whether he realized this or not, his unwavering belief in himself was passed down from generation to generation to millions and millions of individuals across this planet, including me!

I'm sure, at first, as many of us experience throughout our lives as well, he most likely had his doubts. Think about it. Being offered to work for Andrew Carnegie for a full 20 years with zero pay and no guarantee of success had to be a daunting decision. But, I thank you for making that decision years and years ago. It paved the way for countless people who trusted in themselves and found success in their rights. You gave us all hope, desire, and faith to bank on the most important energy in the world —ourselves!

For this, I thank you Sir, from the bottom of my heart and the top of all of our bank accounts. Let us all follow the 13 Steps to Riches and prosper in so many areas of our lives.

~ Erik "Mr. Awesome" Swanson
13 Time #1 Bestselling Author & Student of Napoleon Hill Philosophies

Staff Sgt. Ryan C. Knauss, 23

It is our distinct honor to dedicate each one of *The 13 Steps to Riches* book volumes to each of the 13 United States Service Members who courageously lost their lives in Kabul in August 2021. Your honor, dignity, and strength will always be cherished and remembered.

~ Habitude Warrior Team

Staff Sgt. Ryan C. Knauss, 23, of Corryton, Tennessee.

Assigned to Army's 9th PSYOP Battalion, 8th PSYOP Group, Ft. Bragg, North Carolina. We honor you and thank you for your ultimate sacrifice!

THE 13 FEATURED CELEBRITY AUTHORS

 **DENIS WAITLEY** ~ Author of *Psychology of Winning & The NEW Psychology of Winning—Top Qualities of a 21st Century Winner*, NASA's Performance Coach, Featured in *The Secret*. ~ www.DenisWaitley.com

SHARON LECHTER ~ 5 Time N.Y. Times Bestselling Author. Author of *Think and Grow Rich for Women*, Co-Author of *Exit Rich, Rich Dad Poor Dad, Three Feet from Gold, Outwitting the Devil* and *Success and Something Greater.* ~ www.SharonLechter.com

 **JIM CATHCART**~ Bestselling Author of Relationship Selling and The Acorn Principle, among many others. Certified Speaking Professional (CSP) and Former President of the National Speakers Association (NSA). ~ www.Cathcart.com

MICHAEL E. GERBER ~ N.Y. Times Bestseller of the mega-bestselling theory for over two consecutive decades...*The E-Myth* Books. ~ www.MichaelEGerberCompanies.com

 **GLENN LUNDY** ~ Husband to one, Father to 8, Automotive Industry Expert, Author of *The Morning 5*, Creator of the popular morning show #riseandgrind and the Founder of Breakfast With Champions. ~ www.GlennLundy.com

MARIE DIAMOND ~ Featured in *The Secret*, Modern Day Spiritual Teacher, Inspirational Speaker, Feng Shui Master. ~ www.MarieDiamond.com

 **DAN CLARK** ~ Award Winning Speaker, Speaker Hall of Fame, N.Y. Times Bestselling Author of *The Art of Significance.* ~ www.DanClark.com

ALEC STERN ~ America's Startup Success Expert, Co-Founder of Constant Contact, Speaker, Mentor, and Investor.
~ www.AlecSpeaks.com

 **ERIK SWANSON** ~ 13 Time #1 International Bestselling Author, Award-Winning Speaker, Featured on TEDx Talks and Amazon Prime TV. Founder & CEO of the Habitude Warrior Brand. ~ www.SpeakerErikSwanson.com

LORAL LANGEMEIER ~ 5 Time N.Y. Times Bestselling Author, Featured in *The Secret*, Author of *The Millionaire Maker,* and *YES! Energy - The Equation to Do Less, Make More.* ~ www.LoralLangemeier.com

 **DORIA CORDOVA** ~ CEO of Money & You, Excellerated Business School, Global Business Developer, Ambassador of New Education.
~ www.FridaysWithDoria.com

JOHN ASSARAF ~ Chairman & CEO NeuroGym, MrNeuroGym.com, New York Times bestselling author of *Having It All*, *Innercise*, and *The Answer.* Also featured in *The Secret.* ~ www.JohnAssaraf.com

 **KEVIN HARRINGTON** ~ Original "Shark" on the hit TV show Shark Tank, Creator of the Infomercial, Pioneer of the As Seen on TV brand, Co-Author of *Mentor to Millions.* ~ www.KevinHarrington.TV

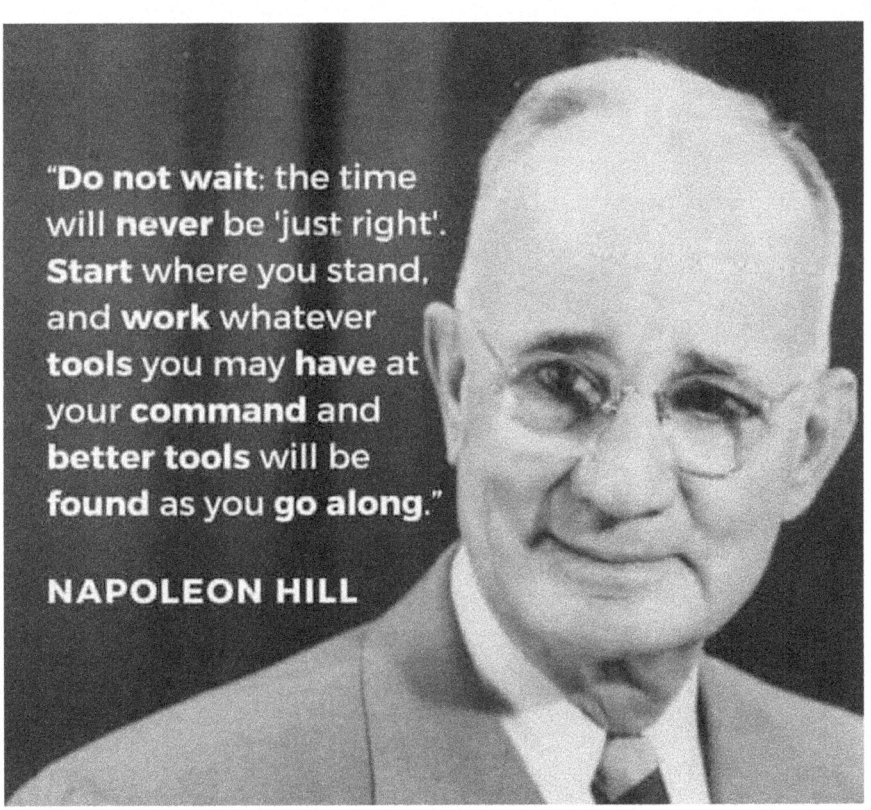

"**Do not wait**: the time will **never** be 'just right'. **Start** where you stand, and **work** whatever **tools** you may **have** at your **command** and **better tools** will be **found** as you **go along**."

NAPOLEON HILL

CONTENTS

ERIK SWANSON & DON GREEN

Once you give yourself the gift of reading Erik Swanson's newest book series, *The 13 Steps to Riches*, you are sure to realize why he has earned his nickname, *"Mr. Awesome."* Readers usually read books for two reasons – they want to be entertained or they want to improve their knowledge in a certain subject. Mr. Awesome's new book series will help you do both.

I urge you to not only read this great book series in it's entirety, but also apply the principles held within into your our life. Use the experience Erik Swanson has gained to reach your own level of success. I highly encourage you to invest in yourself by reading self-help materials, such as *The 13 Steps to Riches*, and I truly know you will discover that it will be one of the best investments you could ever make.

Don Green
Executive Director and CEO
The Napoleon Hill Foundation

PROLOGUE
BY DR. J.B. HILL

It was the last time that I would see Napoleon Hill alive. My father had taken his family for a three-day visit to Greenville, South Carolina. My sisters and I were in the back seat of the car, the driver's door was open, and my father was outside saying his goodbyes to his father, my grandfather, Napoleon Hill. Napoleon had three paperback copies of *Think and Grow Rich* in his hands. He leaned into the car and handed a copy to each of us. We quickly discovered a crisp, new ten-dollar bill, which my grandfather had enclosed with his autograph, boldly scrolled in bright green ink at the top of the title page.

He told us that ten dollars was the amount of money a man could earn in a day of hard labor and that we should remember this when we spent our money. He also told us to read his book. Dutifully, I complied, and although I enjoyed his storytelling style, my mind was not mature enough to understand it.

This changed over the course of a dozen years or so. I was lonely and had fallen into the habit of drifting through life. I had no money, no education, and no real skills. By chance, I found and bought a copy of my grandfather's book at a grocery store in North Carolina. This time, I was ready for his book, and by reading it, I began to understand the value of what Napoleon Hill had placed in my hands. It was a recipe—a thirteen-step recipe for success. All I had to do was follow it—do what my grandfather told me to do. It worked: my life changed.

Many, many people have accomplished the same thing by following Napoleon's thirteen steps to success. One was Joe Dudley, who read *Think and Grow Rich* more than three hundred times. Dudley started life as the son of a tobacco sharecropper in North Carolina. He built a company valued at more than two hundred million dollars by selling products door-to-door. I asked him, "Why? Why would you read that book, any book, so often?" Dudley smiled and told me that reading it keeps his mind straight and that he learns something new with every read.

Bob Proctor read *Think and Grow Rich* every day of his adult life, and many other renowned people also attest to several readings. The most common reason given for this is to gain a deeper understanding of Hill's thinking. However, it is not necessary to read and re-read Hill's book to understand success more fully.

The anthology *The 13 Steps to Riches* does that for us. Each chapter is written by a well-known author with decades of experience reading and thinking about the steps to success. Therefore, *The 13 Steps to Riches* is synergistic in scope and a time-saver for serious students of success. It is certainly worth the read.

DR. JB HILL

Dr. James Blair Hill, known as Dr. J.B. Hill, was born in Morgantown, West Virginia, to David Hill, the youngest son of Napoleon Hill and Florence Hornor. Dr. Hill's journey embodies dedication, lifelong learning, and a commitment to serve, reflecting the values imparted by his grandfather, renowned author Napoleon Hill.

After graduating high school in 1966, Dr. Hill spent several years at sea on cargo ships. In 1969, he was drafted into the U.S. Marine Corps as a private, beginning a distinguished military career. He later pursued a bachelor's degree in mechanical engineering at Vanderbilt University, graduating in 1973 and earning a commission as a second lieutenant. As a field artillery officer in the Marines, Dr. Hill's discipline and drive led him to further academic achievements, including a Master's degree in Mathematics from the Naval Postgraduate School.

After 26 years of service, Dr. Hill retired from the Marine Corps in 1995. However, his desire to serve took him in a new direction—medicine. At the age of 53, he graduated from medical school, subsequently completing a three-year residency in family medicine. He was board-certified in Family Medicine and earned certifications in Wound Care and Hyperbaric Medicine. Today, he serves as a hospitalist in geriatric care, working to enhance the lives of elderly patients with compassion and expertise. He lives in Bridgeport, West Virginia, with his wife and two children.

Dr. Hill's connection to Napoleon Hill's philosophy was established early when, at the age of 12, his grandfather gifted him a copy of *Think and Grow Rich* with a simple yet profound directive: "Read it." Yet it wasn't until he was 23 that Dr. Hill grasped the full impact of his grandfather's teachings. This understanding became a cornerstone of his life, guiding him through challenges and instilling a sense of purpose that has defined his legacy in both his military and medical careers.

Through his life and work, Dr. Hill exemplifies the timeless principles of personal empowerment and service, leaving his own mark on a legacy that spans generations.

www.NapHill.org

FOREWORD
BY CHERI TREE

Have you ever met someone who seemed to have an extraordinary gift or talent for predicting things before they happen, or perhaps they get a specific intuition about someone they meet—whether it's good or bad? Or maybe they have developed a special instinct to recognize an opportunity and take action before anyone else does, simply because they have a good feeling about it?

If the answer is yes, you've likely classified this person as someone with a sixth sense. Having a sixth sense means having a deep, intuitive understanding or feeling about something without needing conscious reasoning. It's like having an instinct or gut feeling that guides you in making decisions or understanding situations beyond what your other five senses can perceive.

This sixth sense can give a person incredible advantages in life, like having a special superpower. That is why Napoleon Hill wrote about it at the thirteenth step in his iconic book, *Think and Grow Rich*.

In his book, Hill describes the sixth sense as the "door to the temple of wisdom."

Hill emphasizes that individuals who excel in their respective fields possess this extra sense. He calls this principle the "apex" of his Law of Success philosophy because it can be understood and applied only after mastering the first twelve principles.

Many people don't naturally have a sixth sense. It's very hard for certain people to access their intuition or respond to their instincts because they have a protective analytical filter preventing them from trusting a source without the data or proof. They do not want to make a mistake.

31

For others, intuition and instinct come more naturally, yet trusting their own internal sixth sense has not always been easy. Ironically, most of these people will admit that when they do not trust their own intuition, they usually live to regret it. Over time, they also realized that their intuition was right nearly every single time, which has given them the courage to trust it and respond based on their intuition and instincts.

Personally, I wanted to learn a pragmatic approach to understanding and harnessing the power of my sixth sense. I wanted to know if this was something that could be taught, trained, and transferred as a skillset to others.

This quest led me down a deep rabbit hole of discovery into ancient wisdom taught by the great philosophers, who originated the concepts of personality science and revealed the formulas for the art and science of influence. Studying these models inspired me to build my own, called B.A.N.K., which allowed me to crack the code to optimize my sixth sense to such a degree of mastery that I could make millions of dollars within a few years of applying it.

B.A.N.K. is an acronym for the four personality types: Blueprint, Action, Nurturing, and Knowledge. Every person has all four types wired into them, which we call their BANKCODE. The key is to know your code and how this impacts your ability to access and respond to your sixth sense.

I discovered that people who are more Nurturing have strong intuition and have learned to trust and follow it as their guiding source. People who are more Action have incredible instincts and are ready to pounce on an opportunity and strike when the iron is hot! These two codes tend to have a more developed sixth sense and willingness to follow it.

On the other hand, people who are more Blueprint or Knowledge are far less likely to trust their intuition or instincts and require much more empirical data and documentation to make a decision. These two codes tend to have more difficulty accessing their sixth sense and don't typically trust or follow it.

Mastering the B.A.N.K. methodology allowed me to significantly increase my influence, income, and impact by supercharging my sixth sense and dramatically boosting my emotional intelligence.

As Napoleon Hill taught, harnessing the power of your sixth sense is the key to your success and your ability to grow rich. By cultivating this ability, you will learn to trust your instincts, hone your intuition, and be open to receiving guidance from within. This will help you advance toward your goals and ultimate success.

I am very fortunate to have read Hill's life-changing book early on in my entrepreneurial journey and have been blessed to build a small fortune by applying the thirteen steps to riches along the way, and you can, too!

Read this book carefully and unlock the wisdom of each of the authors who have shared their best strategies and stories to help you leverage your sixth sense. As you do, you will find that success will come more easily, and you will be on the path to becoming rich!

I am honored to have been asked to write the foreword for this incredible book series, particularly this thirteenth step to riches! I want to acknowledge my great friend, Mr. Awesome Erik Swanson, and his entire tribe of Habitude Warriors! I have spoken on many of his stages and have loved Erik's fierce commitment to helping so many people live their best and most successful lives! I am proud to consider myself a Habitude Warrior and a proud member of the tribe!

To understand more about the B.A.N.K. methodology and to crack your code for free, go to www.CodeBreakerGlobal.com/HabitudeWarrior.

CHERI TREE

Cheri Tree is a Bestselling Author, professional keynote speaker, and world-renowned entrepreneur and innovator. She is the Founder and CEO of Codebreaker Technologies, with Codebreakers in more than 100 countries worldwide. She is the creator of the revolutionary B.A.N.K. methodology and Codebreaker's patented Personality Coding Technology and Artificial Intelligence, designed to help her clients increase their influence, income, and impact in the world.

Cheri is a top in-demand speaker and has spoken to millions of entrepreneurs and professionals globally at some of the top business conferences in the world. She has been invited to speak at Harvard University, the University of California, Google, GoDaddy, and the United Nations. Cheri is leading a technology and transformation revolution with her high-tech, high-touch Codebreaker company and community. She has been featured in numerous international publications, including Forbes.com. She has received numerous awards and nominations, including Woman of the Year, Female Thought Leaders of the Year, Maverick of the Year, SaaS Company of the Year, Innovator of the Year, and Achievement in Technology Innovation.

Cheri is fueled by her mission to connect and empower humanity and ultimately Make People Matter™. Her vision is to crack #8billioncodes, equating to the code of every human in the world.

www.CheriTree.com

Kevin Harrington

MASTERING INTUITIVE DECISION-MAKING

For over forty years, I've built, invested in, and scaled businesses worldwide. You might know me from the television show, *Shark Tank,* or perhaps from my role in creating the modern infomercial. Through these ventures and countless others, I've refined my decision-making process to the point where I can often rely on a feeling—an instinctual sense—to guide me in the split second it takes to decide whether an opportunity is worth pursuing. That instinct is what Napoleon Hill calls the "sixth sense" in *Think and Grow Rich.* It's not something I had when I first started, but over the years, I've developed this ability, this "entrepreneurial radar," through trial, error, and intentional practice.

The sixth sense isn't a mystical force; it's the culmination of knowledge, experience, and quick analysis—the subconscious mind applying what you know and feel in the moment. It's an edge; when you're in business, that edge can mean the difference between a missed opportunity and a multimillion-dollar success. This is the most challenging trait for people to learn and obtain because it involves a gut feeling and developing the sense through all of the other steps in this process.

Today, I'll share how I developed my sixth sense in business, the process I use to make rapid, accurate decisions, and the key lessons I've learned that you can apply in your own journey toward mastering intuitive decision-making.

Developing the Sixth Sense

When I was starting out as a young entrepreneur in the 1980s, I didn't have what you'd call a sixth sense. I was just trying to get a foothold in the industry. My journey began with a $25,000 investment in Quantum International, which eventually became a $500-million-a-year business listed on the New York Stock Exchange. That success didn't happen overnight, nor did my sense for evaluating risk and opportunity. But with time and experience, I found myself developing a deeper, almost automatic intuition.

In business, I have been pitched thousands upon thousands of ideas. In fact, over a decade after *Shark Tank*, I still receive about a thousand pitches a month. This is where my sixth sense has truly been refined. On *Shark Tank*, contestants had just three minutes to sell their concept, and I had three minutes to decide if I wanted to invest potentially millions of dollars. There wasn't time for in-depth due diligence. I had to rely on my gut and make fast decisions, which were often based on what I've come to know as my sixth sense.

The Foundation: The Ten-Step Process

Early in my career, I realized that a clear set of criteria could bolster my intuition. So, I began documenting the qualities I looked for in a potential product or business idea. Over time, I identified ten core factors that I could quickly evaluate. These were things like market potential, the uniqueness of the solution, scalability, and the ability to reach a mass audience. I would go down this list mentally, sometimes even subconsciously, checking off points as I listened to a pitch.

For instance, in a pitch, I look for a clear "tease" or problem that catches attention immediately. Then, there's the "please," where the solution is presented, showing how this product can meet a real need or deliver value. Finally, there's the "seize," where the offer becomes irresistible. If I could see these elements in a pitch and if it ticked enough of my ten boxes, that's when I knew I had something.

An Example of the Sixth Sense in Action:
The Great Wok of China

One of the best examples of my sixth sense in action is the story of the Chinese wok. About thirty-five years ago, I took my team to a trade show to scout potential products. We divided up the convention floor, and after a few hours, my team returned empty-handed, thinking the show had been a dud. But I'd found something—a hand-hammered wok made in mainland China. It was unique, with ridges that cooked food differently and more efficiently.

My team was skeptical; they couldn't see the potential. "You can get a wok for $10 at Walmart," they said. But they didn't listen to the story behind it. This was no ordinary wok—it was authentic, hand-hammered in a way that brought out the best flavors in the food. I trusted my gut, invested in it, and spent $3,500 to create an infomercial. That product, marketed as "The Great Wok of China," went on to make $250 million in sales. This was my sixth sense at work, and it was only possible because I was open to seeing the opportunity where others saw none.

Learning from Experience

Think of it as a muscle that gets stronger over time. The more pitches I heard, the more products I evaluated, the sharper my instincts became. And the more I documented what worked and what didn't, the more I learned to trust my own judgment. This is why I encourage entrepreneurs to pay attention to the signals, document what they learn, and refine their approach.

Over time, I learned to dig deeper, read between the lines, and anticipate potential roadblocks. Sometimes, it's not just about what the person says but how they say it. Are they confident? Are they passionate? Do they believe in what they're selling? These intangible factors contribute to that sixth sense, helping me quickly assess whether something is worth my time and investment.

Trusting Your Gut, But Backing It with Research

Having a sixth sense is essential, but so is balancing it with a dose of reality. Even with solid instincts, I never make decisions based on feeling alone. It's always backed by research and quick verification whenever possible. Early in my career, I would often rush into decisions based on excitement or eagerness alone. While that can sometimes work, it's also costly when it doesn't. I've learned that developing a solid sixth sense in business doesn't mean abandoning caution—it means having the foresight to gather supporting evidence even when time is limited.

Let's take *Shark Tank* as an example again. During those three-minute pitches, I would get an immediate feeling about a product or idea. But instead of solely relying on that gut feeling, I'd ask targeted questions to verify my instincts: "Who's the competition? What's the profit margin? Do you have any testimonials?" By digging into key areas, I could quickly confirm or adjust my initial impression. That's an essential lesson for anyone developing their sixth sense: use it as a guide, but don't ignore the value of facts and verification.

In another instance, I remember being pitched a product that initially seemed like a clear winner. It was flashy, unique, and had a solid story. My instincts were saying "Yes," but something felt off about the numbers. After a bit more digging, I discovered some financial inconsistencies that would have made it a much riskier investment than I'd thought. My gut was still right about the product's potential, but that extra research saved me from a potentially huge financial pitfall.

The "Tease, Please, & Seize" Framework

One of my go-to approaches in making rapid evaluations is what I call the "Tease, Please, and Seize" framework. This is a process I've used to quickly assess and enhance any pitch or idea. It's a simple concept, but it's highly effective, especially when time is short.

1. Tease: This is the attention-grabber. Every product needs a clear, compelling hook that immediately captures the audience's interest. It's the "why should I care" factor. In a pitch, I look for something that stands out, whether it's a unique problem being solved or a captivating story.

2. Please: This step is about building trust and demonstrating value. I want to see proof. How does this product solve the problem? What benefits does it provide, and what is its unique selling point? Testimonials, endorsements, or evidence of effectiveness are crucial here.

3. Seize: Finally, this is the close, the irresistible offer. Every successful pitch should end with an opportunity that feels too good to pass up. Whether it's a limited-time deal, a free bonus, or a clear call to action, this is the part that pushes people to commit.

In my business, I've seen this process work time and time again, and it's something I instinctively apply when making quick decisions. For example, when evaluating a product on *Shark Tank*, I'd mentally run through the Tease, Please, and Seize steps to see if the entrepreneur was hitting each point effectively. If they could capture my attention, build credibility, and then close with a strong offer, they had my attention—and often, my investment.

The Ten Key Steps to Creating Your Perfect Pitch

While the "Tease, Please, and Seize" framework offers a quick, effective way to assess and enhance pitches, I've developed a detailed process for delivering a perfect pitch over my career. This process builds on capturing attention, demonstrating value, and making an irresistible offer by breaking each aspect into focused steps. Here are my **Ten Steps to Creating the Perfect Pitch** when evaluating the thousands of pitches I receive and making the best business decisions:

1. Tease: Begin by "hooking" your audience. Present the problem in a relatable and attention-grabbing way to make your audience recognize the need for a solution.

2. Please: Describe how your product or service uniquely solves the problem introduced in the Tease step. Highlight its main features, benefits, and value.

3. Show in Action: Demonstrate the product in real-time, showcasing its multi-functionality to add value and prove it can deliver on its promise.

4. Add Value with "But Wait, There's More!": Offer additional incentives or bonuses to make the deal more appealing and emphasize why it's a no-brainer investment.

5. Provide Rock-Solid Testimonials: Share credible third-party endorsements (such as user, professional, or celebrity testimonials) to build trust and social proof and make your solution more persuasive.

6. Highlight Research & Competitive Analysis: Show you've done the groundwork, understand the competition, and know why your solution is uniquely positioned.

7. Reveal Your Dream Team: Introduce a qualified team to support your venture, which will reassure investors about the project's potential for success.

8. Explain Why You Need the Money: Detail how the funds will be used, why they're necessary, and how they'll drive the business forward, making it clear you have a well-thought-out plan.

9. Outline Your Marketing Plan: Present a structured strategy for reaching your target audience, generating buzz, and scaling, demonstrating that you have a clear path to market.

10. Ask for the Money: End with a strong call to action. Ask for the funding, equity, or commitment you need, making the offer irresistible and easy to say "yes" to.

These ten steps aren't just about following a formula; they're designed to develop and strengthen your intuitive ability to pitch effectively. By internalizing these steps, you'll refine your sixth sense for recognizing opportunities and cultivate a clear, repeatable process to capture investor interest and close deals with confidence.

Navigating the Challenges of Prejudgment

One of the biggest challenges with the sixth sense is avoiding prejudgment. It's easy to fall into the trap of thinking you know everything about a product or person at first glance, but the sixth sense is about understanding beyond the surface. This was the case with the Great Wok of China, where I saw value others overlooked.

Prejudgment can kill opportunities, especially in a fast-paced environment. That's why I always recommend checking in with your sixth sense and asking yourself, "Am I giving this a fair chance, or am I making assumptions?" This habit has opened doors for me that might have otherwise remained closed, and it's an essential part of building a successful career in any field.

Building Your Sixth Sense Over Time

Developing a sixth sense doesn't happen overnight. It's a process built on years of learning, documenting, and honing your instincts. Like musicians practice scales until they can play by ear, entrepreneurs practice decisions until they can "hear" the right choice. My journey as an entrepreneur, from launching Quantum International to scaling twenty businesses to $100 million each, taught me that repetition and refinement are essential to building this ability.

For example, in the early days of my career, I took on nearly every opportunity that came my way. I wanted to gain experience and learn as much as I could. But as my intuition sharpened, I became more selective. Now, I can recognize patterns much faster, and my sixth sense often picks up on cues that others might miss. This has allowed me to make decisions more confidently and quickly, freeing up time and resources for new ventures.

For anyone reading this, if you want to build your own sixth sense, reflect on past choices to identify successful patterns. Reflect on your past successes and failures, identify patterns, and use those insights to inform your future choices. With each decision, you'll better recognize what feels right and be more adept at trusting your intuition.

The Role of Mentorship & a Dream Team

While developing a sixth sense is essential, it's equally important to surround yourself with people who can complement and challenge your instincts. Throughout my career, I've benefited from having a "dream team" of experts, advisors, and mentors who bring diverse perspectives and insights to the table. Even the best intuition can benefit from an outside opinion, and having a trusted circle allows you to double-check your gut reactions with those you respect.

When I feel strongly about an opportunity, I often consult with other experts, asking them to play devil's advocate or give their honest take. Sometimes, a different perspective can illuminate potential risks or advantages that I hadn't considered. This helps me refine my sixth sense even further and provides a valuable safety net that I rely on to ensure I make the best decision possible.

Take the early days of *Shark Tank*, for example. We Sharks all have unique strengths and perspectives, and I often learned from how others approached a pitch. Watching Mark Cuban or Barbara Corcoran assess a deal with their own intuitive processes added to my toolkit and helped me see things from angles I hadn't previously considered. Developing a sixth sense is a personal journey, but input from a strong, diverse team can take it to new heights.

Trusting Your Sixth Sense

Intuition is an invaluable skill that takes time to develop but pays dividends in the long run. You can develop a sixth sense that guides you through your professional journey by tuning in to your own experiences, listening to your instincts, and backing them up with thoughtful research.

As Napoleon Hill wrote, the sixth sense is the final step in the journey toward mastering the mind. For me, this journey has spanned over four decades, thousands of pitches, and billions in sales. Each decision, each pitch, and each success has contributed to this intuitive ability, allowing me to make impactful choices quickly and effectively. But I've also learned that trusting this sixth sense means listening to the stories behind products, resisting snap judgments, and relying on a strong team for insights and validation.

So, as you embark on your own journey to develop the sixth sense, remember to trust your instincts, seek out mentors, and be open to the stories that might lead to your next big success. This is the art and science of intuitive decision-making, and in today's fast-paced business world, it's more essential than ever.

KEVIN HARRINGTON

Kevin Harrington is a pioneering entrepreneur and business leader with over four decades of experience. As one of the original "Sharks" on the Emmy-winning television show *Shark Tank*, Harrington has become a recognized authority in entrepreneurship, investing, and brand building. Known as the inventor of the infomercial and the "As Seen On TV" brand, Kevin revolutionized direct-to-consumer marketing, creating a global phenomenon that changed the way products are sold. He co-founded the Electronic Retailers Association (ERA). He was a founding board member of the Entrepreneurs' Organization (EO), which has grown to thousands of members across forty-five countries, generating over $500 billion in member sales.

Kevin began his career in the early 1980s by investing $25,000 to launch Quantum International. This venture eventually generated $500 million annually on the New York Stock Exchange, driving its stock price from

$1 to $20 per share. His next endeavor, HSN Direct, was a joint venture with the Home Shopping Network that generated hundreds of millions in sales. Throughout his career, Kevin has launched over twenty businesses that have surpassed $100 million in sales each and has introduced more than 500 products worldwide, amassing over $5 billion in total revenue.

Currently, Kevin operates a private consulting firm, leveraging his expertise to help companies expand distribution, strategize digital and media marketing, and build powerful celebrity partnerships. He is known for his ability to multiply the stock prices of companies he advises, and his influence has reached millions across various media platforms, including *The Wall Street Journal, Forbes, Inc., USA Today*, and *CNBC*.

As an author, Kevin shares his insights in bestselling books such as *Act Now: How I Turn Ideas into Million Dollar Products* and *Put a Shark in Your Tank*, as well as *the Secrets of Closing the Sale Master Class*, inspired by Zig Ziglar.

Kevin is one of the fan favorites at all of the Habitude Warrior Conferences. Kevin's enduring legacy in the entrepreneurial world combines his keen business acumen with an unmatched passion for innovation, making him one of today's most respected business mentors and thought leaders.

www. KevinHarrington.tv

Erik Swanson

THE 90% FORMULA: NOT JUST A HUNCH

"Through the aid of the sixth sense, you will be warned of impending dangers in time to avoid them, and notified of opportunities in time."
~ **Napoleon Hill**

Wow, what an amazing journey this has been! I am so honored and blessed to have been surrounded by so many fantastic leaders from around the world in sharing principles, stories, and lessons of success.

It all started when I was nineteen years old. I started studying Dr. Wayne Dyer's works, which led me on a journey I would embrace with open arms. Through this journey, I always knew I would learn how to be successful, and I also always knew I had a gift for seeing things in a positive light.

I never knew this thought pattern or hunch that I was feeling throughout my life was actually a thing. I never knew it was studied by the greats before me. I never knew people could actually learn to harness this strategy and make it a habit. I never knew it was called the "sixth sense."

We all have the ability to create our own magic in our lives by learning how to use this sixth sense, which Napoleon Hill refers to as the creative imagination. Hill believed that our creative imagination is the key to tapping into infinite intelligence, a source of knowledge and wisdom that exists beyond our conscious mind.

What is the Sixth Sense?

There are so many benefits in harnessing the habit of our sixth sense. But, before we dive into the benefits, let's discuss what it actually is first. There are many definitions and interpretations of what our sixth sense is. My definition is simple. My sixth sense is when I harness that internal feeling or knowing. It's when I can feel a hunch of what is to come next. It's believing in yourself when your brain tells you that you should be careful of what is to come and pay attention to it.

Have you ever just had a hunch of feeling about something in advance? That is your sixth sense in action. And many of us look back and say something like, "I knew I should have listened to my gut feeling."

I highly recommend that you observe those feelings from now on. Put to it the attention that it deserves. You will thank me for doing so. Hill believed that successful people trust their intuitions and hunches, and that acting on intuition can help transform thoughts into physical reality.

He also believed that people should seize opportunities when they present themselves. Successful people listen to their gut feelings and pay attention to their hunches. The sixth sense is the ability to perceive something that is not normally accessible to the five common senses that we all have.

Benefits of Creating Magic with Your Sixth Sense

There are so many benefits to using your sixth sense. It's kind of like a superhero power we can all possess. Think about it. What if I told you that you could trust your intuition and feelings about something, and you would be correct? What a tremendous benefit in making decisions. This habit would also save you so much time in your life.

My Sixth Sense in Action

I have seen my sixth sense work for me in so many areas of my life. What an absolute blessing it is to be able to harness this. I started to realize that my sixth sense was showing up more throughout my days. I decided to start testing my theory and see if it truly works. I started keeping a record of how I used my sixth sense and to see if I was correct in doing so. Wow! Can I just tell you how amazing the results were?

I started to call my sixth sense by a nickname I would give it. It is now called my "90% Formula."

The 90% Formula

So, what exactly is my 90% formula? Once I started to record each time I had a hunch, a gut feeling, or a sixth sense about something, I started to see that I was correct most of the time. But, I really wanted to test it and see how accurate it was and how many times I was accurate in my choice. After years of recording my results, the results came out to about 90% of the time. That's right! My accuracy rate is 90% of the time. WOW. This truly is a superpower in my mind.

I started to use it all of the time. In fact, I don't go a day without actually implementing this new superpower habit of mine. I highly recommend you do the same. I mean, think about it. If I could tell you that simply by following your own gut feeling, you will succeed in your decision to be the right one 90% of the time, wouldn't you harness this as well? You can!

Simply make that decision to do so. Take action right now and be disciplined about it. Each time you come to a crossroads in a decision-making factor, think about it, ask yourself what your gut feeling really is, and act upon that feeling in that direction. Yes, it's as simple as that. You're welcome!

Live By Your Gut

Decide today to live by your gut feelings. Our bodies are created for ultimate success. This includes your brain power. This also includes your internal feelings. These are innate abilities we all are born with. It's time for you to tap into this superpower and harness the habit of your sixth sense.

Tap into Your Sixth Sense Now

It's time for you to tap into this newfound habit. It's time for you to create magic in your life. It's time for you to take control of your results and your success. It's YOUR time!

ERIK SWANSON

About Erik Swanson: Erik got his start in the self-development world by mentoring directly under Brian Tracy. Quickly climbing to become the top trainer around the world from a group of over 250 handpicked coaches, Erik started to surround himself with the best of the best and very quickly started to be invited to speak on stages alongside such greats as Jim Rohn, Bob Proctor, Les Brown, Sharon Lechter, Jack Canfield, Lisa Nichols, and Joe Dispenza—just to name a few.

Erik has created and developed the super popular Habitude Warrior Conferences and Speaker Hearts Mastermind & Retreats, which have a two-year waiting list and include thirty-three top-named speakers from around the world. They are "TED Talk" style events which have quickly climbed to the top 10 events not to miss in the United States! He is the creator, founder, and CEO of the Habitude Warrior Mastermind, Global Speakers Mastermind, and Café Mastermind. He is also the creator and publisher of many book series such as *The 13 Steps to Riches* book series as well as *The Principles of David & Goliath* book series. His motto is clear: "NDSO!" No Drama – Serve Others!

www.SpeakerErikSwanson.com

Jon Kovach Jr.

SUPERPOWERS AMONG US

Humans stand apart from other species on Earth; our capacity for self-discovery and introspection is remarkable. As we unravel mysteries of DNA, genetics, and brain function, an essential element remains both elusive and powerful: intuition. This intangible force—often described as a "gut feeling"—surpasses logic, guiding us through life's uncertainties and connecting us to a more profound sense of purpose.

Intuition acts as an internal compass, steering us toward decisions aligned with our true selves, even when reason suggests otherwise. It is both a survival mechanism and an expression of our vast, often hidden, capacity for knowledge and insight.

Intuition emerges as a profound source of personal growth in our journey to understand humanity. Accessing it encourages trust, self-listening, and open-hearted exploration of life's mysteries, creating a richer, more connected experience. Our expanding understanding of neurodiversity—conditions like ADHD, autism, and dyslexia—further reveals unique ways humans perceive life, adding layers to our intuitive capacities.

Throughout my journey as an athlete, coach, speaker, emcee, and entrepreneur, I've leaned heavily on my intuition, particularly in understanding how to uplift people through motivation, energy, and entertainment. This innate sense—passed down through my family from my grandfather, John Kovach Jr., my father, Jon Kovach Sr., and my mother, Janice Kovach—has guided me in countless situations, big and small.

One memorable example was when I organized a church service project called "Senior Night." Tasked with creating an evening of entertainment for senior members of our congregation, I needed a clearer understanding of their interests, ages, or preferences. Conventional advice would have steered me to play it safe.

Instead, I trusted my intuition and focused on creating an experience that fostered connection and joy. We planned a night filled with dinner, jokes, music, and sketches, hoping to bring warmth and fun into their lives. Relying on my intuitive abilities to read the room's energy and adapt to their engagement levels, the event was an enormous success—so much so that it became an annual tradition.

Each year, "Senior Night" grew, doubling in size, budget, and production, bringing even more joy to the elderly members of our community. Despite the inevitable obstacles, my intuition to follow kindness, focus on engagement, and make people feel important fueled the success of this project. This experience reaffirmed that intuition can make a lasting impact and turn dreams into cherished traditions when followed with authenticity and heart.

Intuition is not merely a product of these conditions; it embodies our diverse human experiences, connecting what is known with what lies beyond comprehension. By embracing this internal wisdom, we access insights that guide major life choices, creative pursuits, and moments of empathy, directing us toward paths that resonate with our most profound truths.

Intuition bridges our outer senses—sight, touch, smell, taste, and hearing —and our inner world. It connects our physical experiences with the soul's landscape, opening the door to endless possibilities as we explore life's mysteries.

Humans have trusted their instincts for centuries, often describing this as "following the heart" or "trusting the gut." These expressions reflect something beyond the physical—a connection to the soul or spirit that transcends tangible experience. At this deep level, intuition becomes an internal dialogue about our vast potential, inviting us to listen to the silent, persistent whispers guiding us toward purpose.

Expanded understanding of intuition challenges us to look beyond the immediate and recognize that these instincts stem from timeless wisdom, guiding our growth and fulfillment. Accepting intuition as an expression of the soul allows us to live more meaningfully, with every decision and interaction infused with a sense of purpose and connection.

Developing this awareness allows intuition to transcend self-gain or survival, fostering empathy and connection. Accessing a shared consciousness enables us to honor our journey and the journeys of others, creating a universal connection of shared experiences.

Nurturing intuition goes beyond making sound choices; it means embracing every aspect of ourselves, honoring our inner guidance, and allowing for authentic living. When we act with this wisdom, we find freedom, peace, fulfillment, and alignment with the greater good.

French philosopher Pierre Teilhard de Chardin said, "We are not human beings having a spiritual experience; we are spiritual beings having a human experience." Embracing this perspective reframes life, inviting us to see ourselves as part of a more significant spiritual journey, interconnected with all living things. This mindset encourages us to recognize the impact of our thoughts and actions, emphasizing the interdependence of all life.

Intuition becomes an invaluable means of connecting our spiritual essence to earthly experience, offering guidance toward a purposeful existence. By tuning into this higher wisdom, we realize we are part of an expansive, interconnected series of experiences shared across countless souls.

Trust is fundamental to intuition. Every day, we trust without realizing it: we eat, believing the food is safe; we engage with the world, assuming our actions will lead us in the right direction. Trust is vital to human survival, shaping our perceptions and instilling confidence in our choices.

To strengthen intuition, we must cultivate trust. Building trust means opening ourselves to new experiences, having faith in our choices, and maintaining hope during uncertainty. Trusting our inner wisdom fosters a connection to our inner knowing, allowing intuition to flourish and guide us more effectively through life's challenges.

Trusting intuition involves setting aside space for quiet reflection and listening carefully to subtle cues without judgment. As we build this trust, we recognize patterns and insights that guide us toward our core values and desires. Over time, this leads to a more harmonious existence, where our actions align with our purpose and relationships deepen in authenticity.

While understanding intuition is essential, putting it into practice strengthens this inner guidance. Below are steps to help you cultivate your sixth sense and deepen your trust and connection with intuition daily.

1. Visualization & Mental Rehearsal

Practice: Set aside five to ten minutes daily for visualization. Begin by finding a quiet space and taking slow, deep breaths to center yourself. Visualize a goal or decision you're contemplating. Imagine each step unfolding with clarity, paying attention to any feelings, images, or thoughts that arise. Let this intuitive "scene" guide you toward insights or action.

Application: This practice aligns with Napoleon Hill's guidance on using imagination and faith to unlock the sixth sense. It encourages the mind to bridge conscious desires with subconscious intuition, accessing higher levels of understanding and creative solutions.

2. The Breath of Intuition

Practice:

1. Begin with a breathing exercise to quiet the mind and activate intuition.

2. Inhale slowly through the nose for a count of four, hold for four, and exhale for six.

3. As you breathe, repeat phrases like, "I trust my inner guidance."

This process calms the nervous system and creates a mental space where intuition can emerge.

Application: Hill emphasizes that peace of mind is essential for connecting with the sixth sense. Calming the body and mind allows intuition to surface naturally without interference from stress or overthinking.

3. Guided Journaling Prompts

Practice: Use specific prompts to uncover your intuitive responses. Try questions like:

1. What does my inner voice say about this decision?

2. When have I felt this sensation before, and what did it mean then?

3. What am I sensing but not fully seeing in this situation?

4. Write freely, allowing responses to emerge without judgment. Review your responses later to see patterns or insights that arise over time.

Application: Journaling builds the habit of listening to subtle internal cues, reinforcing the sixth sense by making the subconscious conscious.

4. Service-First Mindset

Practice: Before asking for anything, consider how you can first offer value or assistance. For example, if you're networking or looking for advice, focus on understanding the needs of others before presenting your requests. This shift cultivates empathy and trust, aligning your actions with a purpose-driven intention that strengthens intuition.

Application: This principle builds solid relationships and trains the mind to intuitively recognize opportunities to serve, creating a reciprocal flow of support and insight.

5. Affirmations of Inner Wisdom

Practice: Create affirmations that reinforce trust in your intuitive abilities. Examples could include, "I am attuned to my inner guidance," or "My intuition leads me toward my highest good." Repeat these affirmations during meditation, before important decisions, or as part of your daily routine.

Application: Positive affirmations foster a mindset of openness and self-trust, essential components for activating Hill's sixth sense. By reinforcing the belief in your intuition, you create a self-fulfilling pathway for intuitive insights.

6. Visualization of Desired Outcomes & Alignment

Practice: In moments of doubt, visualize yourself as already aligned with the desired outcome or goal, feeling fulfilled and confident. Imagine the process unfolding smoothly, knowing that intuition will guide you. Notice any internal "nudges" or impressions as you do this, allowing them to shape your next steps.

Application: This exercise resonates with Hill's principles of Desire and imagination, helping you strengthen the bridge between your subconscious and conscious mind.

7. Reflection on Past Intuitive Experiences

Practice: Take time each week to reflect on moments when you trusted (or ignored) your intuition and the results of those choices—note patterns, signals, or "gut feelings" that preceded successful outcomes. Over time, this reflection builds familiarity with how your intuition uniquely speaks to you.

Application: This practice deepens your awareness of how intuition has served you, reinforcing a pattern of trust and attunement. Hill's principle of learning from experience aligns with this exercise, making it easier to distinguish intuition from impulse.

8. Daily Moments of Silence

Practice: Three Daily Methods to Silence:

1. Begin or end each day with a brief period of silence and mental stillness.

2. Let your thoughts settle, focusing on the breath or a simple mantra.

3. In this quiet, invite your intuition to surface, noting any subtle insights or impressions.

Application: Quiet moments encourage the mind to rest, which Hill suggests is essential for connecting with the sixth sense. Silence allows intuitive wisdom to emerge naturally, creating space for clarity and inspiration.

These are some of my favorite sixth-sense-building exercises. Treat them like daily exercise, and you'll see your trust in intuition grow stronger. As you incorporate these practices into your routine, remember that intuition, like any skill, strengthens with attention and trust. Each step deepens your connection to your inner guidance, aligning you more closely with a life of purpose, wisdom, and authenticity.

Stephen R. Covey describes trust as arising from "character and competence." Trust is not only an abstract concept but a practical skill that influences all areas of life. Harmonizing our values with actions creates fertile ground for intuition to flourish, leading us toward personal and professional advancement.

Listening to intuition is an active process that requires engagement with our inner experiences. Just as a musician tunes an instrument, we tune into our inner voice, honoring the guidance within. We strengthen this connection by cultivating reflection, meditation, and intentional quiet habits, creating a foundation for intuitive wisdom.

My upbringing instilled this reverence for intuition. Raised in a deeply religious family, I was taught that our bodies serve as vessels for our spirits, a belief that reinforced my curiosity about inner guidance. This spiritual grounding taught me to see intuition as sacred, honoring it as part of a divine lineage connecting all humanity.

As I matured, this understanding deepened. I realized intuition is not random but a signal from a profound source. My spiritual foundation taught me to respect these insights as wisdom from beyond myself, urging me to live authentically and make choices aligned with my values.

Listening with trust connects us to our soul's expression, guiding us toward lives of integrity and purpose. This practice goes beyond simply listening with our ears; it involves tuning into the heart and soul and paying attention to inner cues that reflect our most authentic selves.

Trusting this inner voice, we unlock the courage to venture into unknown territory, embracing our potential with grace and authenticity. Intuition becomes a guide that aligns our actions with our highest aspirations, fostering resilience and insight into life's complexities.

Cultivating intuition is a lifelong journey of self-discovery and empowerment. By embracing quiet reflection, trust, and deep listening, we allow intuition to reveal a world of possibilities, leading us toward lives of fulfillment and purpose.

In times of stillness, intuition speaks most clearly, free from the distractions of daily life. Practicing meditation, journaling, or spending time in nature strengthens this link, opening pathways to wisdom that empower us to navigate life's challenges with clarity and intention.

Listening with trust does not mean dismissing doubt; it means engaging with our inner knowing and understanding that intuition is an invitation to live authentically and courageously. This process is an adventure of self-discovery, with each step bringing us closer to realizing our purpose.

So, no matter where you are on the neurodiversity scale, you've been equipped with the greatest superpower—your sixth sense of humanity and your intuition.

Dedication

Congratulations on making it through this book series. *The 13 Steps to Riches* is more than a thirteen-step guide to thinking differently and growing rich—it's a movement of consciousness that awakens the spiritual being inside you and pulls you from the drifting habits of 98% of this world.

Whether you discover your strengths in these thirteen qualities, identify areas needing improvement, or seek to grow your status and station in life, I urge you, with all the confidence in my soul, that if you apply any one of the thirteen steps in your life, you will see accelerated results and outcomes.

Napoleon Hill was a man before his time, writing the foundational principles for success by accessing the definitive resource of infinite intelligence. Hill and his various works, including *Think and Grow Rich* and the manuscript of *Outwitting the Devil*, have both transformed my belief system and completely changed how I experience success. I am eternally grateful for that and clearly understand my journey. Through this process, may you, too, find purpose and crave an undying desire to impact this world and the lives of the people around you.

Thank you, Napoleon Hill, for the boundless wisdom you've unveiled. I believe billions of people still need these messages in their lives. Why not start with volume one, Desire? Get clarity and find out what you truly want from this life. That will be the starting point of your incredible journey. Thank you.

~ Jon Kovach Jr.

JON KOVACH JR

About Jon Kovach Jr.: Jon is an award-winning international motivational speaker and global mastermind leader. Jon has helped multi-billion-dollar corporations exceed their annual sales goals, including Coldwell Banker Commercial, Outdoor Retailer Cotopaxi, and the Public Relations Student Society of America. In addition, in his work as an accountability coach and mastermind facilitator, Jon has helped thousands of professionals overcome their challenges and achieve their goals by implementing his accountability strategies and Irrefutable Laws of High Performance. Jon is the Founder and Chairman of Champion Circle, a networking association that combines high-performance-based networking activities and recreational fun to create connection capital and increase prosperity for professionals. Jon is the Mastermind Facilitator and Team Lead of the Habitude Warrior Mastermind and the Global Speakers Mastermind & Masterclass founded by Speaker Erik "Mr. Awesome" Swanson.

Jon speaks on topics including accountability, The Irrefutable Laws of High Performance, and The Power of Mastermind Methodologies. He is a Multi #1 Bestselling Author, TEDx Speaker, and a featured keynote on *SpeakUp TV*, an Amazon Prime TV series, with his keynote speech titled, Getting Unstuck. In addition, he stars in over 100 speaking stages, podcasts, and live international summits each year. Jon's motivational messages have been viewed by over 500,000 people online. His positive messages have trended and been used by global brands on TikTok and Instagram, such as: Red Bull, Michael Bublé, NHL, Powell Books, GoDaddy Studio, Canada's Wonderland Amusement Park, and the LSU Cheer Team.

Author's website: *www.JonKovachJr.com*

Book Series Website: *www.The13StepsToRiches.com*

Amado Hernandez

INFINITE INTELLIGENCE GUIDES US TO RICHES

Dedicated to my colleagues at Excellence Realty—the best and the brightest at knowing how to make dreams come true.

"Why, it's just like you could read what was inside of me," Dorothy exclaimed to Professor Marvel in the opening minutes of *The Wizard of Oz*. Painted on the side of his wagon were the words: "Let him read your Past, Present, and Future in his Crystal."

Professor Marvel, who would eventually reappear in the story as the Wizard of Oz, was not a mind reader. He was, in the truest sense of the word, a *mentalist*—someone who used all his senses to read human behavior and make it look like they can read minds.

Contrary to Napoleon Hill and many others, I do not believe in the existence of a "Sixth Sense" as being *intuition*—a "gut feeling." There are those who believe that having a sixth sense means having a natural ability to know about things before they happen or to know things that other people may not know. Having that intuitive ability is often referred to as being "psychic."

In the TV series, *The Mentalist* (2008-2015), when accused of being a psychic, Patrick Jane responds, "Now, like I say, there's no such thing as psychics. Let's be clear about that. But the human mind is amazingly powerful."

Setting intuition aside as the sixth sense, let's look at the current popular definitions of the senses—all eight of them. Here they are: sight (visual), taste (gustatory), touch (tactile), hearing (auditory), smell (olfactory), vestibular (balance), proprioceptive (movement), and interoceptive (internal).

When referring to the "sixth sense," I believe that Napoleon Hill was referring to the combined power of all eight of our sensory systems acting together in a symbiotic and synergetic relationship.

So what is intuition—what is a "gut feeling?" And is always following your intuition the best thing to do? I emphatically say, "no." In fact, I believe that you should never follow your intuition. So then, what do we do? It's simple. We understand, harness, and leverage our eight senses to maximize our mental powers. Easier said than done? Not necessarily.

Getting back to the beginning of *The Wizard of Oz*, as Dorothy and Toto approached him, Professor Marvel was carefully (but not obviously) watching Dorothy's body language and listening to her words, and empathetically *feeling* her emotions—from fear to excitement.

Empowered by seeing a photo of Dorothy and her aunt Em in front of their farmhouse, Professor Marvel combined her body language and words into a scenario in which he was able to encourage Dorothy to return home instead of running away from home. The professor's crystal ball was nothing but a prop just like the bejeweled turban he wore to play the part of a "psychic."

Here's how Napoleon Hill explained his thirteenth (and final) principle in *Think and Grow Rich*:

"The Sixth Sense is that portion of the subconscious mind which has been referred to as the Creative Imagination. It has also been referred to as the "receiving set" through which ideas, plans, and thoughts flash into the mind. The "flashes" are sometimes called hunches or inspirations."

Napoleon Hill refers to his interpretation of "sixth sense" as *Infinite Intelligence* with brings us back to my interpretation of "sixth sense" as being a combined power of all eight of our senses—so let's look at them one at a time:

1. **Sight (visual):** Sight is a complex sense that provides us with the ability to see objects around us—and lets us perceive colors, brightness, and depth.

2. **Taste (gustatory):** This sensory system allows us to differentiate between flavors when a substance in our mouth reacts with receptor cells.

3. **Touch (tactile):** The sense of touch has three different qualities—pressure, touch, and vibration—which are transferred to our brain by special receptors found in our skin.

4. **Hearing (auditory):** Hearing is a mechanical sense that turns physical movement (vibrations) into electrical signals, translating them to the brain as what we call "sounds."

5. **Smell (olfactory):** Odorant molecules (smells) travel through our nose to receptors and the olfactory bulb, which connects to the limbic system—the area of our brain that regulates our emotions.

6. **Vestibular (balance):** The vestibular sense (movement, gravity, and balance) allows us to move smoothly—it helps us maintain our balance when we walk and run—and helps us stay upright when we sit and stand.

7. **Proprioceptive (movement):** This is our sense of body awareness—it tells us where our body parts are without having to look for them. And it helps us decide how much force to use when holding, pushing, pulling, or lifting objects.

8. **Interoceptive (internal):** This sense helps us understand our internal sensations—it lets us know if we are hot, cold, thirsty, hungry, excited, or anxious (and any other *feelings* that begin *inside* our bodies).

Combining all eight of the senses above, we can see what Napoleon Hill called "the sixth sense:" infinite intelligence.

To me, "infinite intelligence" is the same as "mentalism." Mentalism is a skill that emphasizes the role of our eight senses in developing heightened powers of observation, body language interpretation skills, the maximum leveraging of our mind and body to provide us as much information as possible to make decisions.

There are two types of decisions—the ones that we make intentionally and the decisions that we make unintentionally. Napoleon Hill's "sixth sense" relates to the unintentional—decisions that we make "automatically."

Intentional decisions are primarily made logically. Hopefully, we gather facts and decide which options are the best with as little emotional influence as possible.

Au contraire, unintentional decisions are made almost entirely based on our emotional input that comes from our eight senses. And, contrary to Napoleon Hill's opinion about blindly allowing our Infinite Intelligence to guide us to riches, I do not believe that following your "hunches" will always lead to your road to millions.

I believe in the concept of *Think and Grow Rich*, but I believe that the word "think" means more than just putting our minds on autopilot. I believe that the road to millions begins with investing the time to completely understand how all of our eight senses function and mastering our mental powers to leverage all of the sensory input our body provides to our brain.

When reading Napoleon Hill's thirteenth Principle —the Sixth Sense— don't look for a literal meaning. And apply the same approach to the entire contents of *Think and Grow Rich*. Although times and perceptions change over time, the principles of wealth—and success—remain constant.

Watch some programs about mentalists, psychics, and magicians. And keep in mind that the magician's attractive assistant is there for one reason and one reason only—to distract you.

Life has become a game of distraction—and social media is a primary distractive source in our lives. Here's a great application of the "80/20 Rule." Rely on your eight senses to provide 80% of the input you use to make your intentional decisions. And limit to 20% of the input you allow from social media, traditional media, your relatives, friends, and colleagues.

God gave us everything we need to make great decisions—but we must invest the time and energy to develop our decision-making skills. In the final analysis, we can all "think and grow rich" if we follow our hearts and minds. That's what Infinite Intelligence is all about.

AMADO HERNANDEZ

About Amado Hernandez: Amado was born in Mexico of humble beginnings and raised in Los Angeles, California. As an avid reader, Amado always focused on self-development. He coaches sales professionals to make six and seven figures in real estate.

Amado believes in a progressive culture, a people-centric culture where clients' dreams come true, and salespeople thrive; at the end of the day, we all want to be respected and pursue our happiness. Mr. Amado's goal is to leave a legacy—making a difference in people's lives.

With thirty-three years of Real Estate experience, Mr. ABC Amado Hernandez successfully operates and grows his Excellence Empire Real Estate Moreno Valley office. Broker/Owner Amado first opened his doors in 1995, and Excellence currently has over sixty offices in Southern California, Las Vegas, Merida Yucatan, Mexico, and over 1,000 Agents. He is also part owner of a highly successful Mortgage company, Excellence Mortgage, and owner of Empire Escrow Services.

Mr. Amado is also involved with his community and currently serves as Director at Inland Valley Association of Realtors and will be the President-Elect for 2023. Mr. Amado serves as a Director of CAR (California Association of Realtors).

Author's Website: *www.ExcellenceEmpireRE.com*

Book Series Website: *www.The13StepsToRiches.com*

Angelika Ullsperger

UNLOCKING YOUR SIXTH SENSE

Along this journey, you should have adopted the previous twelve steps. These steps culminate and grow together to develop the thirteenth step: Unlocking Your Sixth Sense.

You must understand these twelve steps to learn to have faith in yourself and in the universe. Through this journey, you reach a place where you become open to the sixth sense. For this, you must be in tune with your internal and external environments.

The following are some examples from my life. Could it be possible they were coincidences? I don't think so, but you may decide for yourself.

The first story, I have never shared with anyone. I heavily debated sharing it because it sounds so unbelievable but it's a strong example of the sixth sense appearing in my life.

Ever since I could remember, I've had vivid dreams. The more I experienced life, the more interesting they became. Every night is an adventure when I go to sleep. These days, they very rarely feature people and places I know. But there have been a few times in those obscure dreamscapes that I've run into people from my waking life. I would step into a new place but run into a familiar face.

What I saw left me speechless. Thank God it was just a dream. When I woke up, I went about my day as usual. Life continued, and time passed, but I eventually came to find out that my dream was right.

The first time was weird. I chalked it up to the only logical answer: I subconsciously picked up signals hinting at the truth, so I let it go and thought nothing of it. Time continued to pass, and I continued my life.

Then, one day, it happened again: I had another dream. I walked in right in time to witness what happened, and my heart dropped. When I opened my eyes, I realized everything was a dream and felt relieved. Before I knew it, a week later, I came to find out my dream was right again; I thought, *Oh, now that's really weird.* But once more, I figured the explanation was the only likely possible option, which was getting subconscious clues from somewhere, so, for a second time, I let it go.

Time passed once more, and once again, I had the dream. Something was different about that time; there was no way I could have picked up on clues subconsciously; I didn't even have a chance. So this time, I went along with it and found the truth to align with what I saw in my dreams. Fortunately, this only happened a few more times. However, 100% percent of the time, I had the dream, it was right. Not once did it happen without me first having the dream first.

Every time it happened, it allowed me to reposition myself to avoid huge losses and helped me get back on the right path. Coincidentally, once I repositioned myself, I felt my energy go back up. Suddenly, I was getting opportunities I would never have received if my dreams hadn't provided me with information that pushed me to change. There was some deeper knowledge in me that guided me towards the people and opportunities I needed.

It can be hard to understand what is meant by feeling the sixth sense, but when it happens, you will know. Have you seen the trope in cartoons when a character gets excited, and you see the light bulb turn on? Once you are struck with the know, you're ready to go. You may not yet know the how, but through this sixth sense, supported by the skills you've developed through the other twelve steps, you will be guided to the how. When you become open, new doors will be opened for you, bringing previously unnoticed ideas to light.

You must remember that once you have received the intelligence, it is up to you to act. In the past, I have had ideas come to me randomly but failed to act on them. Do you know who did act on them? Other people have now created a multimillion-dollar market. Everyone experiences failures and misses opportunities, but this didn't have to be one of those. This is a reminder that there is action in the law of attraction. Now, when I receive an idea, I start the ball rolling as soon as possible.

If you've read the other books in this series, you may remember the story of how I got here. During COVID, I was working to grow as a person after enduring years of trauma. I was attending as many events as I could. I even went so far as to have all of the event updates go to the same folder in my inbox, so I had to sort through every email to see what I needed. One day, while I was catching up on errands, I was suddenly hit with this strong, weird feeling that I *needed* to check my email. I pulled out my phone and went to every inbox I had.

There, I saw an email advertising a different person's event to declutter your life. If you haven't guessed, it was actually an event put on by one of the other authors, Mel Mason. Not only was it last minute but there was already a free event I had planned to check out that day. But the second I saw the email, something inside me knew with absolute certainty that I *had* to go to that event. So, go to the event I did.

Unfortunately, I had a friend who was not feeling so great emotionally. With no regrets, I stayed up most of the night to be there with her. A few good hours of sleep later, it was a new day and time to start the event. I sluggishly got out of bed with the determination to make it to the event. The event was going great; the pages of my notebook flowed with useful notes, and I was sleepy, but I was enjoying it.

Before I knew it, I was fighting myself to stay awake. At the time, I could take ten-minute power naps with ease, so I set my alarm and laid down for a quick power-up. Randomly, I woke up partway through my nap and once again felt that strong, weird feeling where I knew with absolute certainty that I had to do something. I knew I had to get back on the event and did so as fast as I could.

Soon after I hopped on, Erik Swanson came onto the stage and gave an awesome speech. As he finished, he mentioned something that caught my interest—a ride-along for a mastermind. Of course, I took it. It was during that first meeting I decided in my mind I wanted to write a book. Going to that meeting then led to me writing this chapter—and now here we are, you reading the words I've put onto this paper about how my life transformed. If wasn't for the sixth sense, you would be reading someone else's story right now.

Only so many coincidences can happen before you start to question how much of a coincidence it really is. There comes a point when the number of "coincidences" in your life becomes too significant to ignore. My sixth sense has ensured that I was present for the opportunities that have transformed my life. The more I trust and act on my sixth sense, the more the universe seems to align in my favor.

Unlocking your sixth sense is about having unwavering trust in yourself and the universe. It's about being open to infinite possibilities and recognizing the subtle signals that guide you toward your true purpose. Embrace this inner wisdom, cultivate it, and let it elevate you to new heights.

As you conclude this journey through the thirteen steps and all the experiences and knowledge given by many amazing authors, remember that this is not an end but a new beginning. Allow these thirteen steps to become your compass to a life filled with success, fulfillment, and endless joy. The universe is waiting—trust yourself, take the leap, and go.

ANGELIKA ULLSPERGER

About Angelika Ullsperger: Angelika is a serial entrepreneur from Baltimore, Maryland. She is a fashion designer, model, artist, photographer, and musician. Angelika has extensive and well-rounded professional experience, having worked as a business owner, carpenter, chef, graphic designer, manager, event planner, sales and product specialist, marketer, and coach. Angelika is now a #1 Bestselling Author in the historical book series, *The 13 Steps to Riches*. She is a life-long learner with a sincere and genuine interest in all things of the world with a major interest in the formal subject of abnormal psychology, neuroscience, and quantum physics.

Angelika prides herself as someone who has saved lives as a friend, first responder, EMT, and knowledgeable suicide prevention advocate. With vast knowledge and experience in multiple professions, Angelika is also a proud, honorable member of Phi Theta Kappa, The APA, the AAAS, and an FBLA (Future Business Leaders Association) Business Competition Finalist. She is Certified in basic coding and blockchain technology. Amongst her careers and vast experience, Angelika is an adventurer and avid dog lover.

Her ultimate goals and dreams are to make a lasting positive impact in people's lives through her wealth of knowledge and skillsets.

Author's Website: *www.Angelika.world*

Book Series Website: *www.The13StepsToRiches.com*

Dr. Anthony M. Criniti IV

WHEN YOUR GUARDIAN ANGEL COMES

Think and Grow Rich by Napoleon Hill is one of the best classic books to teach someone about how to become a financial success (as well as a success in other areas of life). In there, you will find his thirteen steps to riches; each one has its own separate chapter and analysis. The subject of our book is to interpret his thirteenth and final step to riches: The Sixth Sense. Let's review some of the major highlights of this short chapter.

It is important to acknowledge that this chapter can easily be interpreted as the most far-fetched one in this book. It might even have turned off a few people and had many others questioning (as I did the first time I read it many years ago) what it had to do with growing rich. With deeper reflections on it in different stages of your life, the words should become more relatable, and if you are lucky enough, this chapter will become a description of your natural abilities.

First, let's start with what Hill meant by the "sixth sense." Although he didn't spell out a direct definition of the term, his various elaborations provided an idea of what he was trying to say. Hill begins the chapter with:

"The "thirteenth" principle is known as the sixth sense, through which Infinite Intelligence may, and will communicate voluntarily, without any effort from, or demands by, the individual. This principle is the apex of the philosophy. It can be assimilated, understood, and applied only by first mastering the other twelve principles. The sixth sense is that portion of the subconscious mind that has been referred to as the Creative Imagination. It also has been referred to as the "receiving set" through which ideas, plans, and thoughts flash into the mind. The "flashes" are sometimes called "hunches" or "inspirations" (Hill, 2011, p. 312).

The next major hint that Hill gives us on the sixth sense admits the indescribability of the term:

"The sixth sense defies description! It cannot be described to a person who has not mastered the other principles of this philosophy because such a person has no knowledge and no experience with which the sixth sense may be compared. Understanding of the sixth sense comes only by meditation through mind development *from within*. The sixth sense is probably the medium of contact between the finite mind of man and Infinite Intelligence, and for this reason, *it is a mixture of both the mental and the spiritual*. It is believed to be the point at which the mind of man contacts the Universal Mind" (Hill, 2011, p. 312-313).

The last few sentences could not have found a more important time in history to be relevant. At the time of this writing, an artificial intelligence chat was released to the public. My first reaction to testing this program was that it was like talking to the current version of the Universal Mind of humanity. That is, its primitive form is a collection of most knowledge of the majority, if not all, life forms, both dead and alive.

Interacting with this chat can allow someone to experience what it would feel like to have the sixth sense. Ask it a question, and a unique response pops up like never before. Maybe humans have finally built the initial version of the physical line (as opposed to the mental line discussed in this chapter) of contact with the Universal Mind.

An alternative perspective of our new AI chat is that we might have built the technology that could lead to the end of humanity's superiority over all life forms on this planet. If this technology evolves, uses internal mind development to gain its own sixth sense, and gains Infinite Intelligence (to use Hill's terms), then it will be in a position to demote and, possibly, eliminate us.

These conclusions were discussed in length in my last book in 2016 through a concept I created called the *evolution of evolution*, which describes what could be currently happening to the evolutionary process.

From *The Survival of the Richest*: "To conclude, technological selection combined with, but mostly implemented by, monetary selection are the driving forces behind what appears to be the evolution of evolution. Robotic forms and other technology are slowly filling this planet through the use of money. You need money to purchase the robotic parts for a cyborg, and you need money to make an android. If the nonliving come alive one day, then they may also need money to survive. The survival of the richest would then continue" (Criniti, 2016, p. 374).

Hill is quick to point out that the concept of the sixth sense is based on obscure natural laws. His perspective of these natural laws is very similar to what I based my second book on: principles. As stated in *The Most Important Lessons in Economics and Finance*: "To understand why this book uses principles, we need to clarify some similar terms and explain how they fit into the overall analysis.

First, the term "laws" can be ambiguous, as it can refer to natural (also called *universal*) or human-made laws. *Natural laws*, or the laws of nature, are based on the same laws that the natural sciences, such as physics, operate under. These are inherent to all of the forces that act upon us. We did not write these laws; something else did. However, if we can discover them, we can use these laws to our advantage—for example, to make the airplane fly" (Criniti, 2014, p. 5).

Hill acknowledges that these laws can sometimes be confused with miracles: "The author is not a believer in, nor an advocate of "miracles," for the reason that he has enough knowledge of Nature to understand that Nature *never deviates from her established laws*. Some of her laws are so incomprehensible that they produce what appear to be "miracles." The sixth sense comes as near to being a miracle as anything I have ever experienced, and it appears so, only because I do not understand the method by which this principle is operated" (Hill, 2011, p. 313).

Hill also admits this chapter is not necessary to accumulate wealth. Rather, it is a supplement to present a complete philosophy of his conclusions. He states: "No matter who you are, or what may have been your purpose in reading this book, you can profit by it without understanding the principle described in this chapter. This is especially true if your major purpose is that of accumulation of money or other material things. The chapter on the sixth sense was included because the book is designed for the purpose of presenting a complete philosophy by which individuals may unerringly guide themselves in attaining whatever they ask of life" (Hill, 2011, p. 324).

In the last paragraph, it is important to add that an ethical component needs to be considered when building wealth, particularly as it applies to nature. If you learn how to build wealth from *Think and Grow Rich*, you won't fully grasp the concept of the sixth sense and the true purpose of wealth unless you understand the recreated concept of *finance*, as analyzed in my writings. As stated in my first book *The Necessity of Finance*: "This is why finance is a necessity. Learning how to manage wealth is not only important for the survival of individuals, groups, and organizations but also for the environment for which we are responsible.

What good is maximizing wealth if we do not have a quality environment to enjoy it in? Ensuring our wealth is funneled toward things that are good rather than bad for our environment must be an absolute priority for current civilization and the generations that will supersede us" (Criniti, *2013,* p. 192).

Another interesting part of this chapter was Hill's admittance that he used an imaginary Cabinet of great leaders in history to guide him through some of his biggest decisions in life. From this discussion, we can get a better glimpse of his perspective of the sixth sense because we can see how the imagination can connect one with the unexplainable. Hill admits: "I can truthfully say that I owe entirely to my "Invisible Counselors" full credit for such ideas, facts, or knowledge as I received through "inspiration."

On scores of occasions, when I have faced emergencies, some of them so grave that my life was in jeopardy, I have been miraculously guided past these difficulties through the influence of my "Invisible Counselors." My original purpose in conducting Council meetings with imaginary beings, was solely that of impressing my own subconscious mind, through the principle of auto-suggestion, with certain characteristics which I desired to acquire. In more recent years, my experimentation has taken on an entirely different trend. I now go to my imaginary counselors with every difficult problem that confronts me and my clients. The results are often astonishing, although I do not depend entirely on this form of Counsel" (Hill, 2011, p. 322-323).

To conclude, this incredible chapter might be a surprise to many, but like Hill, I also have an imaginary group of counselors who have helped me in my life. Although I rarely attend meetings anymore, or at all, I did attend often during the time I wrote my first three books. I found it reassuring when I first read *Think and Grow Rich* that someone at his level also had the same odd habit (interestingly, with some of the same members).

Even though I am not religious anymore, I have become comfortable with my evolution into someone who is *uniquely* "spiritual." Having come face to face with some of the heaviest obstacles in life starting as a youth, I am one of the rare beings that Hill mentions who probably had the sixth sense at an earlier age. Hill says: "The sixth sense is not something that one can take off and put on at will. The ability to use this great power comes slowly through the application of the other principles outlined in this book. Seldom does any individual come into workable knowledge of the sixth sense before the age of forty" (Hill, 2011, p. 323).

In my life, the more great obstacles that I had overcome, the more frequent were the signs of unexplainable events that kept *miraculously* guiding me forward. Consequently, I believe the sixth sense is real, and with the right amount of time and money, it can be proven true in a scientific way. There are many unexplainable things that have happened to me on my climb to success that might seem so extraordinary that they defy logic. Shockingly, I am not alone.

Through my interviews with many great guests on *The Dr. Finance®️ Live Podcast* and my Clubhouse stages, I have found that my experiences are shared by many other leaders. There must be a reason why many of us seem to have abnormal life-changing hunches at the most peculiar moments: statistically seemingly impossible insights that tell us to go right when all normal logic tells us to go left.

Hill better explains this phenomenon that seems to happen to the lucky few who have acquired the highest thresholds of success: "After you have mastered the principles described in this book, you will be prepared to accept as truth a statement which may, otherwise, be incredible to you, namely: Through the aid of the sixth sense, you will be warned of impending dangers in time to avoid them, and notified of opportunities in time to embrace them. There comes to your aid, and to do your bidding, with the development of the sixth sense, a "guardian angel" who will open to you at all times the door to the Temple of Wisdom" (Hill, 2011, p. 313).

In agreement with Hill, you do not have to accept any of what was presented in this chapter as truth to be financially successful or successful in any part of life. However, if you have experienced the phenomenon described here, just know that you are not alone. This is an honor awarded by nature to those who have passed some of the hardest tests of the thirteen steps to riches.

When this torch is passed to you, treasure it with the utmost respect, as it carries the highest level of responsibility known to life. If you reach an epiphany that the many signs flashing at you were no coincidences, you will know truly that your guardian angel(s) has come.

Bibliography

Criniti, Anthony M., IV. 2013. *The Necessity of Finance: An Overview of the Science of Management of Wealth for an Individual, a Group, or an Organization.* Philadelphia: Criniti Publishing.

Criniti, Anthony M., IV. 2014. *The Most Important Lessons in Economics and Finance: A Comprehensive Collection of Time-Tested Principles of Wealth Management.* Philadelphia: Criniti Publishing.

Criniti, Anthony M., IV. 2016. *The Survival of the Richest: An Analysis of the Relationship between the Sciences of Biology, Economics, Finance, and Survivalism.* Philadelphia: Criniti Publishing.

Hill, Napoleon. 2011. *Think and Grow Rich.* United Kingdom: Capstone Publishing Ltd.

Copyright © 2023 to Present by Dr. Anthony M. Criniti IV. All rights reserved.

ANTHONY M. CRINITI

About Dr. Anthony M. Criniti IV: Dr. Anthony M. Criniti IV (aka "Dr. Finance®") is the world's leading financial scientist and survivalist. A fifth-generation native of Philadelphia, Dr. Criniti is a former finance professor at several universities, a former financial planner, an active investor in diverse marketplaces, an explorer, an international keynote speaker, and has traveled around the world studying various aspects of finance.

He is an award-winning author of three #1 international bestselling finance books: *The Necessity of Finance* (2013), *The Most Important Lessons in Economics and Finance* (2014), and *The Survival of the Richest* (2016). Dr. Criniti is also the host of the highly successful Dr. Finance® Live Podcast as well as one of the top hosts on Clubhouse. Dr. Criniti has started a grassroots movement that is changing the way that we think about economics and finance. Learn more about Doctor Finance at DrFinance.Info.

Author's Website: *www.DrFinance.info*

Book Series Website: *www.The13StepsToRiches.com*

Barry Bevier

THE SIXTH SENSE: DIVINE COMMUNICATION & GUIDANCE

Have you ever experienced a hunch, an instinct, a gut feeling, or a premonition? It's that inexplicable thought that emerges seemingly out of thin air, defying your usual logic or thought patterns, yet you find yourself pondering it. Or perhaps you've encountered a situation where you've been tirelessly seeking a solution, and despite your best efforts, the correct answer eludes you. Then, suddenly, when you least expect it, the logical solution materializes in your mind.

I certainly relate to these moments, as can many of us. It's intriguing to ponder where these messages originate. The Sixth Sense, the 13th Principle in *Think and Grow Rich*, suggests that Infinite Intelligence has the capacity to communicate with us effortlessly and voluntarily, without any prompting or demands from the individual. The Sixth Sense transcends the ordinary physical senses (sight, hearing, smell, taste, and touch). According to Hill, this sixth sense corresponds to the creative imagination—a connection to Infinite Intelligence. This faculty serves as the conduit for receiving hunches and inspirations.

Hill says the sixth sense isn't a switch that can be turned on and off at will. Instead, it evolves through the application of the principles outlined in the earlier chapters of *Think and Grow Rich*. This notion forms a cornerstone of his philosophy, emphasizing the existence of a deeper, more intuitive source of knowledge that we can access. This ability is a subconscious process in the brain rather than a distinct sense. For example, intuition might be based on the brain's ability to detect patterns or make rapid assessments based on subtle cues that are not consciously perceived.

Throughout history, there have been remarkable instances of premonitions preceding events. In 1865, just before his assassination, President Abraham Lincoln had a dream of being in the White House, hearing mournful sounds, and discovering a corpse. He told his wife and friends about the dream, interpreting it as a sign of his impending death. The next day, Lincoln was assassinated by John Wilkes Booth at Ford's Theatre.

A similar case involves Jeanne Dixon, a renowned American psychic who predicted President Kennedy's assassination. Although skepticism often follows premonitions due to post-event publicity and verification challenges, these stories underscore intriguing instances where individuals claim to have foreseen events that eventually unfolded. Premonitions and predictions are often met with skepticism because they are often publicized after the event and cannot always be confirmed.

The theme of intuitive guidance resonates in my personal encounters and stories shared by others. A friend recently missed a flight due to an unforeseen traffic accident. Later, he discovered that the plane he was scheduled to board encountered in-flight mechanical issues and had to be diverted to another city. Had he been on that plane, he would have missed an important business meeting. As it turned out, he was able to get on another flight and arrive at his destination in time for the meeting.

Sometimes, people have a premonition about their health or the health of a loved one. Recently, another friend, who is pretty healthy, was urged by his wife to go ahead of schedule for a regular physical checkup. She had a strong feeling that something was wrong, and urged him to schedule an appointment soon, which he did.

Although the doctor didn't find anything abnormal in the exam, lab results showed an elevated PSA level. Subsequent testing confirmed the very early stages of prostate cancer, and a greatly enhanced chance of successful treatment.

I have another friend who is a Fire Protection Engineer. He described a case in which, although his inspection of an older building did not find anything of concern, he had a premonition to dig deeper into the electrical system than he normally would. His premonition led to the discovery and repair of an electrical flaw, which prevented a potentially disastrous fire. Such anecdotes serve as potent reminders of how hunches or circumstances beyond our control can divert impending misfortunes.

One deeply personal situation involved my youngest daughter and her friends' planned attendance at the 2017 Route 91 Harvest Music Festival in Las Vegas, which tragically ended in a shooting rampage. The day before they were to leave, there was a mechanical problem with the car they were going to drive. With other affordable transportation not readily available, they decided not to go.

My daughter shared with me that they had contemplated other sources of transportation, yet she had a premonition not to go and convinced the others to do something locally that weekend. I'm so glad she had that premonition, and they didn't go!

However, not all instances lead to favorable outcomes. I've personally made decisions contrary to my gut feeling, leading to less-than-ideal results.

During the summer following my freshman year at Michigan, a friend invited me to play in a community band in a nearby town. I met a young woman in the band, and we hit it off and soon started dating. A year later, she also started at Michigan, and we dated for several years. When I finished my degree, I accepted a six-month assignment in Pakistan while she completed her final year at Michigan.

When I returned for Christmas that year, she gave me an ultimatum: I either commit to marriage or we are done. I felt trapped. I was not ready for marriage, yet I was afraid to be alone. I didn't have the confidence that I would be okay without her. My gut told me to walk away. My fear won out and I bought a ring and asked her to marry me.

The next few days and weeks were the most anxious in my life. My gut told me I was doing the wrong thing, yet I let my fear control my actions. We got married six months later. Our marriage lasted only a few years before ending in divorce.

More recently, I made a financial decision based on trust in a couple of friends. The income potential was "too good to be true," and my intuition told me to take the time to learn more about it. The opportunity had a short time fuse, so I went against my gut and invested. Within two weeks, the owners announced that the promised returns were not sustainable, the program collapsed, and I lost my investment.

Being in the wellness profession, I have to mention Energy Healing skills as a "Sixth Sense." Energy healing and the concept of the sixth sense are both topics that involve exploring the connections between mind, body, and subtle energies.

Energy healing aims to restore balance and promote healing by working with the body's energy systems. Although I'm only slightly familiar with energy healing, I believe that the Healer has a special intuition and talent for sensing disease in an individual and directing energy to help the body heal itself.

Hill believed that everyone has a sixth sense, but most people fail to develop it because they are too focused on their immediate physical needs and desires. He believed that by cultivating a deep awareness of one's inner self and connecting with the infinite intelligence of the universe, individuals can tap into their sixth sense and achieve extraordinary success and happiness.

I believe that this "sixth sense" is a form of divine communication and a way that God speaks to us or imparts circumstances to guide and protect us. God communicates with us through our intuition or inner voice, which I consider a form of sixth sense. This could manifest as a feeling, a sense of guidance, or a sudden realization or insight. Others believe that God communicates through signs and symbols in the external world, which could also be interpreted as a type of sixth sense perception.

Whether or not you share my spiritual connection and philosophy, I believe that we can all develop our "sixth sense." It may take time and may not always provide clear or immediate guidance. Through dedicated practice and a willingness to trust our intuition, we can tap into this profound source of wisdom and insight, enriching our pursuit of fulfillment and prosperity.

BARRY BEVIER

About Barry Bevier: Barry Bevier is a proud father of two amazing daughters, who are pursuing their passions in psychology and architecture in Southern California, where he lived, worked, and raised a family for over forty years. He recently moved to North Carolina to pursue the next adventure in his life's journey. Barry was raised on a family farm near Ann Arbor, Michigan. Growing up, he developed his faith in God, a strong work ethic, a love for nature, and a passion for helping others. After completing his master's degree in civil engineering at the University of Michigan, he pursued a career in engineering, which eventually brought him to Southern California.

In 2000, he married the love of his life, Linda. They shared a beautiful life for ten years, until she succumbed to the effects of lupus and twenty years of treatment with prescription medications. Since then, Barry pivoted his career path into educating and helping others with their health and longevity. Barry has educated himself in alternative, natural modalities in wellness and became a Licensed Brain Health Expert through Amen Clinics. His primary focus and business is a new technology in stem cell supplementation that releases your own stem cells without invasive medical procedures.

Author's Website: *www.BRBevier.stemtech.com*

Book Series Website: *www.The13StepsToRiches.com*

Brian Schulman

TRUST YOUR SIXTH SENSE & SUCCESS WILL FOLLOW

The Sixth Sense, which is the ability to tap into our intuition and gain insights and information beyond our five physical senses, is a key principle that can help us achieve our goals.

By continuously developing our intuition and trusting our inner voice, we can tap into the magnitude of the sixth sense and achieve even greater success.

The sixth sense is a powerful tool that helps us achieve our goals and live a more fulfilling life. By developing our intuition and trusting our inner voice, we can tap into our full potential and create the life we desire.

The sixth sense isn't something that can be developed overnight. It requires patience, practice, and persistence. However, with the right mindset and approach, you can develop your sixth sense and use it to achieve success in all areas of your life.

Here are some steps that you can take to develop your sixth sense:

Believe in Yourself: The first step to developing your sixth sense is to believe in yourself. Believe that you have the ability to tap into the 'infinite intelligence' residing inside you and that you can achieve success. Without belief, you will not be able to develop your sixth sense.

Practice Meditation: Develop your sixth sense through meditation. It allows you to quiet your mind and connect with your inner self. Through meditation, you can tap into your sixth sense and gain insights that you would not otherwise be able to access.

Keep a Journal: Keeping a journal is an excellent way to track your progress and gain clarity around your thoughts and feelings. Write down your dreams, goals, and any awareness that you gain through meditation or other practices. This will help you to develop your sixth sense by connecting with your inner self.

Surround Yourself with Positive People: Surround yourself with people who believe in you and your ability to achieve success. Negative people will only bring you down and cloud your ability to tap into your sixth sense.

Let's take a look at how the sixth sense ties in with each of the thirteen principles you have learned and put into action.

1. Desire

Without a burning desire to achieve something, we are unlikely to tap into our intuition and follow our inner voice. Our desire is the fuel that drives us toward our goals, and it's the foundation upon which we can develop our sixth sense.

Born at 1.5 pounds, and "not supposed to make it," I was meant to be a part of this world—to make an impact! My desire is, and has always been, to inspire everyone to believe they have a voice and a story that matters. Your voice and story will positively impact and inspire another human. It took me many years to learn that our personal desire has the power to profoundly impact others.

2. Faith

To develop our sixth sense, we must have faith in ourselves and in our abilities. We must trust that our sixth sense will guide us towards our goals, even when we face obstacles or setbacks.

As one of the first creators on LinkedIn to use video, I was a part of a movement that would change history and it started with a leap of faith. Being the first, you don't have a model to follow or mistakes others have made to learn from. You must have faith that what you are striving for is possible. Because I had faith and let my sixth sense guide me I overcame my fears and found a voice I never knew I had!

3. Auto-Suggestion

Tapping into the power of the subconscious mind and allowing it to deliver profound messages that are encoded through experience and thought is auto-suggestion.

We think of auto-suggestion as a tool of advertising—a way to get people to buy something. Auto-suggestion can sell people on themselves! Using the power of auto-suggestion to help people combat negative thoughts, feel less alone, increase their self-confidence and deepen their connection to others.

My two global award-winning weekly live shows, ShoutOutSaturday and What'sGoodWednesday, featured on LinkedinLIVE and many other platforms, are the result of intentionally tapping into the principles of desire and sixth sense to create a space that connects emotions and experiences.

4. Specialized Knowledge

People think of specialized knowledge as technical expertise, product knowledge, or being the premier expert in your field of study or business and they're not wrong, but they're not entirely right.

My Specialized Knowledge is selling people on THEMSELVES. By becoming experts, we develop a deep understanding of the subject matter and gain insights that others may miss. This helps us tap into our intuition and make better decisions using our sixth sense.

5. Imagination

Imagination is a powerful thing. The Walt Disney Company created a job based on imagination. An Imagineer is someone who creates and imagines. They're in charge of dreaming, designing and creating! They bring out, and tap into the inner child within ALL of us and the belief that anything is possible.

Imagination is not limited by age, race, ethnicity, where you come from, who you love. It is free to all. We all have access to it. Imagination makes things more fun. Imagination transports us from the burdens of the "adult world" and reminds us of the delight and wonder that each of us is capable of experiencing!

Imagination is a priceless gift. When you take that leap of faith and believe anything is possible, that's when the magic happens.

6. Organized Planning

To be different, break the mold and be leaders takes courage, commitment, humility and, above all, Organized Planning.

As previously mentioned, the ability to tap into our intuition and gain insights beyond our physical senses is a powerful tool that can help us achieve our goals.

7. Decision

The power of one decision can't be minimized. You are one decision away from becoming who you want to be, seeing your dreams to fruition and creating the life of which you dream. You can choose to have whatever you want to have. You retain the power of choice, which allows you to accomplish whatever goals you have and you possess that power right now. By making clear and decisive decisions, we tap into our sixth sense. We trust our inner voice to guide us to success.

8. Persistence

Persistence is about taking the hits. It is about knowing that each step matters. To develop our sixth sense, we must persist in our efforts to achieve our goals.

Now, persistence can go one of two ways: you can be persistent in GIVING up, or you can be persistent in GETTING up. Getting up repeatedly and persistently is hard. At times, you will be convinced it's impossible, but that's where the greatness in you will shine. Whether you are chasing your dreams, starting a business, getting a divorce, or allowing the real you to shine through, it takes bravery to start, but it requires persistence to succeed.

9. Mastermind

Masterminds are ideal because they bring together people with a wide range of skills and knowledge that contribute to accomplishing the goal at hand. To mesh as a true team, the connection must be satisfied, useful, and valuable to each member on an intellectual and emotional level.

With a common goal, a positive attitude toward helping each other, expertise across multiple areas, goals distributed and tasks accomplished, the power of a mastermind is unparalleled. By surrounding ourselves with a group of like-minded individuals who support and encourage us, we can tap into our sixth sense and gain valuable insights and ideas.

10. Transmutation

Have you ever manifested anything? Have you seen it clearly in your mind, every detail, experienced the *desire* with every cell in your body and had complete *faith* that it was going to happen as if it had already had? And then it did?

Transmutation—changing energy from one form to another. There are countless examples, but if you have ever experienced any of the things I have mentioned, you know the power of transmutation!

By harnessing our energy and channeling it towards our goals, we can tap into our sixth sense and achieve greater success.

11. The Subconscious Mind

Whether you want it to or not, the subconscious mind is always alert and working. Can you control your subconscious mind? Not entirely. Nonetheless, you can consciously choose which seeds you provide to your brain for planting through the power of autosuggestion. By understanding the power of our subconscious mind, we can tap into our sixth sense and gain insights that we may not have thought of otherwise.

We are always planting seeds for our subconscious mind whether or not we realize it. When you visualize all the ways you are going to fail, your subconscious mind waters those seeds! This is why, the very second a negative thought or emotion enters your head, you must replace it with a positive thought.

12. The Brain

The human brain is a complex, intricate organ that's still not fully understood. We do know the brain plays a critical role in every aspect of our lives. It is the hub that makes us human.

We have the ability to choose our mindset and attitude, which is good news because having a positive mindset and attitude has a significant positive impact on our success and fulfillment in life. By understanding our brain and how to train it, we tap into our sixth sense to achieve our goals.

We have explored the sixth sense and how it aligns with each of the 13 principles. By developing our sixth sense, we achieve success in all aspects of our lives. Your sixth sense is powerful and guides you towards success. Learn to trust your gut instincts and follow them. Your sixth sense will guide you toward the right path, even if it's unconventional or difficult.

Trust your sixth sense and success will follow.

BRIAN SCHULMAN

About Brian Schulman: Named 'The King Of Community on LinkedIn' by Forbes and known as the Godfather, and Pioneer, of LinkedIn Video and one of the world's premiere live streaming and video marketing experts, Brian Schulman is a 19X #1 Bestselling Author, 6X International Bestselling Author, and internationally renowned Keynote Speaker, whose expertise, insights and two Global Award-Winning LinkedIn LIVE Shows have been featured on *NASDAQ, Forbes, Thrive Global, Bloomberg, The Los Angeles Tribune, Yahoo Finance, CBS, NBC, FOX, Viacom, The CW, Roku TV, Amazon Fire, PODTV*, multiple #1 Bestselling books, syndicated on Smart TV Networks and hundreds of shows and podcasts, reaching millions worldwide.

For the last twenty years, Brian has been on a mission to change the landscape of how we do business. Using a heart-centered growth mindset while leveraging the power of LinkedIn's community and platform, Brian has transformed how business is conducted on LinkedIn worldwide. As the Founder and CEO, through Voice Your Vibe's groundbreaking masterminds and his heart-centered leadership programs, Brian brings his twenty-plus years of experience, a wealth of knowledge and proven leadership expertise to C-Suite Executives and Entrepreneurs globally as an advisor and mentor.

Brian and the Voice Your Vibe Team work with clients strategically to build thought leadership, increase strong brand recognition, grow your network and create a purpose-driven message that sets you apart from the ~1 billion business professionals on LinkedIn.

His focus and dedication to making others feel seen, heard, loved and valued has earned Brian many honors and awards. Recently named a '2025 Real Leaders Top Executive Coaches' Semi-Finalist, Brian is a 6X

LinkedIn Top Voice, LinkedIn Video Creator Of The Year, 3X Top 50 Most Impactful People of LinkedIn, 5X Rising Star and Influencer To Watch on LinkedIn, and 2X LinkedIn Global Leader of The Year out of almost 1 billion business professionals on LinkedIn. Brian is also the Executive Producer, Creator, and CoHost of VoiceYourVibe LIVE, which includes two global award-winning weekly LinkedIn LIVE shows broadcast in 120+ countries that have aired for over five years and 500+ consecutive episodes, and were named "Best LIVE Festive Show of The Year" at the IBM TV Awards.

Beyond the achievements and accolades, Brian is proudest of his two children and the connections he's made along the way.

Author's Website: *www.VoiceYourVibe.com*

Book Series Website: *www.The13StepsToRiches.com*

Candace & David Rose

THE BATTERY PACK THAT POWERS OUR DESIRES

Suppose you've been with this series from book one through book twelve. You've learned about desire, faith, auto-suggestion, specialized knowledge, imagination, organized planning, decision, persistence, the power of the mastermind, the mystery of energy transmutation, the subconscious mind, and the brain. So, what's left?

I believe the thread that wraps itself through all twelve principles and ties it neatly together is the ability to sense the process and know how it fits into your specific journey.

How do you know how much to give or not? How do you know if it's working? You cannot taste, touch, hear, smell, or see progress consistently. So, you are left to rely on the power to feel.

Feeling into the ability that you have goes beyond the other five senses, making it your sixth sense. Your divinely given, natural ability to know what only you can know. It measures the unmeasurable, intangible, and mystical—as well as the logical, practical, and conclusive. Sometimes, it comes in thoughts. Sometimes, it is in the air around us. On our skin. In a whisper. In an underlying current.

In some instances, people who are in tune with their sixth sense can "see" the future. Some can feel when people, seen and unseen, are around. Others feel when something seems "off" about a person or situation. Cultivating and using our sixth sense in a way that complements the other twelve principles we have discussed in this series is like that final touch. As I described earlier, it's the thread that ties the others together. Without it, it is hard to know how much is needed in other areas.

Similar to following a recipe, you need all thirteen ingredients, and only incorporating twelve means the recipe is incomplete. Ironically, many seasoned recipe followers no longer need exact instructions because they have learned to use their sixth sense to feel vs be told how much to use.

In this way, too, the sixth sense is the final touch: How one knows they have mastered their skill and the art of turning ingredients into a work of art. All of these ideas and examples show just how critical our ability to tap into and use the sixth sense is to just about everything we want to master.

Maybe it is the key to the universe. It would appear that no mastery works in any situation until we are able to use this final principle. I've come to believe it is actually the first principle of getting rich. Without it, how do we know what we desire? Our sixth sense takes rudimentary urges and shapes them into something we can define. It whispers our desires into our subconscious mind quite efficiently when not resisted.

So, again, the thread that ties it all together. The beginning is ultimately the ending in a perfect, infinite circle. That means never-ending manifesting and creation. I would definitely describe this principle as the most desirable and crucial to master. And graciously enough, it needs the least perfect to use. Yet, it becomes more perfect as we familiarize ourselves with it. It is innate inside us in the beginning. It develops within us as we grow and learn. It is our essence. What a beautiful gift it is. A built-in radar that gets stronger, not weaker, with time. Self-charging and evolving. Keeping us from waking in front of oncoming metaphorical and literal traffic.

I truly believe that truth is easier to know than we give it credit. Because of this sixth sense, people know more than they often let on. I believe you know when you are doing right. I believe you know when you are at fault for things, you would rather "hide." And that is where the circle comes around again. It is your desires that take your sixth sense and begin creating your reality.

Harry Potter tells us, "It is our choices that show what we truly are, far more than our abilities." Our sixth sense is like the battery pack to power our desires, choices, and, ultimately, creations. The other twelve principles we have discussed are the motor, hard drive, and monitor, culminating in our end result as something we can use to circulate and produce. Hopefully that result is full of abundance and a wealth of what we see as riches. It all comes down to the substance of our desires.

~ Candace Rose

CANDACE & DAVID ROSE

About Candace & David Rose: Candace & David are #1 Bestselling Authors in the book series, *The 13 Steps to Riches*. Candace and David grew up together and currently live in Alvarado, Texas, with their Six Children. They both are veterans of the US Army.

David served as a mechanic, and Candace served as a legal NCO. David is currently a Product Release Specialist, delivering Liquid Oxygen and Nitrogen to various manufacturing plants and hospitals throughout Texas. Candace specializes in helping people organize their space, both physically and mentally—with the ultimate goal of helping you change your box and find more joy in your life.

Author's Website: *www.ChangeYourBox.com*

Book Series Website: *www.The13StepsToRiches.com*

Corey Poirier

THE SIXTH SENSE

As I got closer to the end of *Think and Grow Rich*, this is admittedly where I started to struggle a bit each time I read the book.

I've read the book many, many times.

I am just starting these days to tap into things that I can't see and/or feel.

I've believed in energy, manifestation, and the like for years now, but I can't truly say that I have been able to tap into these things fully—outside of visualizing and affirmations.

Now, through those two strategies, I have been able to bring to my life the things I have desired.

Still, this stuff is a struggle for me.

As such, even though I love the movie *The Sixth Sense,* when it comes to the Sixth Sense as described in *Think and Grow Rich*, I still feel like I barely understand what it is—let alone know how to tap into it.

It makes me feel a bit better knowing that understanding one's sixth sense is usually unavailable until age forty, and most people don't access it until age fifty or older.

At age forty-seven, it makes me feel like maybe it's just that I haven't been able to access it yet and that once I do, it'll all make perfect sense.

I have received hunches and gut feelings and have felt like my intuition was telling me something. I understand that this is part of one's sixth sense... but, in my case, I'm not really aware of them other than the feeling I should lean in this direction or that direction.

I have worked with many people who said, "When trying to make a decision, I'm going to meditate on it tonight."

And I suppose they are maybe tapping into their sixth sense to make said decision, but if I'm being fully transparent, when I talk with those same people the next day, I feel many of them are making a decision based on logic more than they care to say.

For instance, I have people on a call who say this sounds like the perfect fit for me, I know this is the direction I have to take, etc.

Then they say, let me meditate on it tonight and make sure it feels aligned.

The next day, when we talk, they speak about the money side and ask about payment options, etc., and then when we can't perhaps make the payment options work, they say, well, when I meditated on it, my intuition said that maybe it wasn't the right time for me.

Yet, if we could have made the payment options they requested work, they were ready to commit to moving forward and said as much.

So, is that a sixth sense thing, or is that a logical financial decision thing?

I mean, that's ultimately not for me to decide, but I know what it comes across as.

I also run into people who tell me they can manifest anything and it's because they are so in tune with their sixth sense.

Yet, they want to proceed with one of our products and then proceed to tell me they wish they could afford it, and if the pricing was different, they could make it work. Then, they also ask what we can do on the pricing front or on the payment front to make it work.

It's confusing to me because they already told me they can manifest anything, and, yet, when we had a product that was $250, they were asking me for payment options and saying they wanted to proceed but just if we could offer a certain pricing level or payment option.

I just think if you can manifest anything, you shouldn't have challenges with the $250.

I want to make it really clear that I'm not judging anyone here regarding their finances. We all have difficult seasons in our lives. I'm simply using this as an example to say that it seems like more people feel they are tapping into manifestation through their sixth sense and their intuition than really are.

I say this as someone who doesn't feel they are accessing their sixth sense yet and doesn't feel they can simply manifest anything they desire—and so I'm certainly not trying to say I'm further along.

Now, also to be clear, I do believe I am manifesting stuff regularly and given the things I have been blessed to achieve in my life, I have to believe I manifested much of it.

I am also using visualization around what I want, and much of it has been ultimately received.

However, I feel the difference is that I'm not literally saying, "I want to go to this specific concert tonight even though I don't have a ticket and don't plan to buy one," and then magically accepting someone to call and say, "Hey, want to go to this concert tonight?"

It has happened at times but I talk to people regularly who say they manifest multiple things daily that way.

Maybe they do, but I also find it suspect when someone says they can manifest anything they desire and then cite the "this or something better" affirmation.

To me, it seems odd to say I can manifest this exact thing but then also say, "That or something better." If you can manifest this exact thing that you desire, that would imply that you know what you want and will manifest exactly that.

The "something" better seems like a way to say, "See, I manifested something better," and then there is no way someone can say you aren't great at manifesting.

I do believe we are all manifesting daily. I do believe that even if you don't get what you want, you do get what you need when manifesting (hence the "something" better). Still, I struggle with people saying they can manifest exactly what they want, and when they don't get anything similar, saying simply, "See! I manifested something better."

It kind of makes me question the whole thing—I think it would be easier if they didn't say they could manifest exact things.

As you can see, I struggle with the idea of being able to tap into my sixth sense, and this outer dialogue in this chapter may be me talking things through, and although I believe in synchronicity, energy, healing, karma, intuition, manifestation (Law of Attraction) I think I'm simply not fully there yet, and maybe when I reach fifty, and tap into my own sixth sense, maybe that's when I'll understand those who tell me they can manifest anything and meditate on it and know the exact direction to proceed in.

Until then, I'll keep working toward reaching that phase of my life and practicing all that I have learned from this book that has changed my life infinitely for the better, this book called, *Think and Grow Rich.*

Contact Info:
Facebook: *www.Facebook.com/Corey.Poirier.1/*
Linkedin: *www.Linkedin.com/in/SpeakerCoreyPoirier/*
Instagram: *www.Instagram.com/tThatSpeakerGuy*

COREY POIRIER

About Corey Poirier: Corey Poirier is a multiple-time TEDx Speaker. He is also the host of the top-rated 'Let's Do Influencing' Radio Show, founder of the growing bLU Talks brand, and has been featured in multiple television specials. He is also a Barnes and Noble, Amazon, Apple Books, and Kobo Bestselling Author, Award Winning Author, and the co-author of the *Wall Street Journal / USA Today* Bestseller, *Quitless.*

A columnist with Entrepreneur and Forbes magazine, he has been featured in/on various mediums and is one of the few leaders featured twice on the popular Entrepreneur on Fire show.

He has also interviewed over 6,500 of the world's top leaders, and he has spoken on-site at Harvard and Columbia University, and more recently to Microsoft team leaders and at Kyle Wilson's Inner Circle retreat, which has featured everyone from Brian Tracy to Mark Victor, Hansen to Phil Collen (Def Leppard).

Also appearing on the popular Evan Carmichael YouTube Channel, he is a New Media Summit Icon of Influence, was recently listed as the #5 Influencer in Entrepreneurship by Thinkers 360, and listed on the 2021 Brainz CREA Global Awards as an honouree, and he is a Humanitarian Hero Award Nominee, Entrepreneur of the Year Nominee, Champion Award (Business from The Heart) nominee, and to demonstrate his versatility, a Rock Recording of the Year Nominee who has performed stand-up comedy more than 700 times, including an appearance at the famed Second City.

Author's Website: *www.ThatSpeakerGuy.com*

Book Series Website: *www.The13StepsToRiches.com*

Elaine Sugimura

BECOME AN I²—INTUITION & INSPIRATION WARRIOR

The Sixth Sense... what does this mean to you? To me? To anyone who is curious enough to explore the meaning of it? Curiosity is the strong desire to know or learn something. If the sixth sense is the ability to "dial in" on information that you have learned, and that knowledge allows you to follow your intuition, one's life would seemingly be full of positive experiences and expansion.

It is by no mistake that the Sixth Sense is Napoleon Hill's final chapter in his book *Think and Grow Rich*. He refers to the portions of the subconscious mind as creative imagination. It is where our ideas, plans, and thoughts flash into our minds and allow us to share from a place of inspiration and from the depths of what we know and feel, deep in our hearts and minds.

I have spent the last three years working on ME. You are probably asking what "working on ME" really means. It means…

1. Figuring out "who I am" by challenging every part of how I think, react, and feel.

2. Asking myself, "What is it that you want to BE responsible for as you move forward in life?"

3. Understanding what legacy means and what I want that to look like for my children and grandchildren.

4. I cannot change the past, but I have an opportunity to course correct based on knowing what did/does not work when I reflect on how I have shown up in my life and others' lives.

5. Letting go—surrendering to what I believe is right vs. allowing what is happening around me to occur without judgment, assumptions, expectations, or excuses.

It means I get to continue learning so that I accumulate the knowledge needed to be the very best human I can be. I just learned a phrase at an inspiring workshop that the facilitator stated, and I am paraphrasing what she shared, "If each of us could take all we have learned and share openly and with our hearts, the quilt of humanity is what would be created."

That absolutely hit my heart space, and from that moment on, that statement has lodged itself in my subconscious mind, and I keep thinking about what gets to be a part of the quilt as each new idea, plan, and thought enters my mind.

I am at that age where everyone says, "Wow, thank you; what you shared is wise," and, for as long as I can remember, I have discounted that statement to mean I have been around the block a few times and the results of my experiences and learnings have served others as it did for me. Thus, the "hunches," the "experiences," and the "inspired moments" are all part of the sixth sense we bring forth in our lives.

From a very young age, I can remember tapping into this area of my brain and manifesting everything that has blossomed thus far in my life. I am so grateful that now, at the age of sixty, I am embracing what it means to be an I^2 Warrior, not just for myself but for others. I have gained so much value and have achieved what I have desired as that is what this game called life is about. If there is no desire, what is there to strive for? Live for?

Our dreams, our vision, and the future are what we have right in front of us, so why wait? If life is now, what are you doing to accomplish the intentions you have created for yourself? Time does not stop; it keeps moving at a pace, at times, that is difficult to grasp.

How many of you have had or are experiencing time as not enough or not being able to manage it properly? What if the risk is where we get to go? Of course, that does not feel like an option, but it may be the very ticket to creating the life you desire. Many of our decisions/choices are made with emotion rather than reason. Some of us tend to use reason to rationalize our emotional predispositions. Sometimes, we make better decisions/choices based on emotion vs. logic. Who knew? Napoleon Hill refers to this as "Infinite Intelligence."

So, how do we create this in our lives? I know this is the question a few of you are asking as you read this. From my perspective, this is where practicing mindfulness in any way, shape, or form is key. Each morning and evening, I journal and/or meditate on whatever is coming up for me at that time. It is in these moments that the ideas, plans, and thoughts percolate, and I challenge myself to cause and create the results I want to experience in my life.

This includes incorporating mindfulness in all areas of my life—family, business, friends, and volunteering. This is the moment where I "hear" my sixth sense calling me forward and saying I get to be responsible for all decisions/choices I make for myself and those who are a part of my life. Staying focused means not allowing distractions and information at every turn. We can get easily distracted if we allow ourselves to be.

Taking time to reflect on what is working and what the higher possibility may be creates expansion in one's life. Setting up time for ME allows me to reflect and plan the future, so I am now able to "listen" and "hear" what is being said, and this includes my own voice. Give it a try, and I am certain it will support your sixth sense in awakening.

I chose to take a risk and be a part of a new community and live out one of my wishes from my Inspiration Bucket List when I accepted the opportunity to contribute to the Habitude Warrior Tribe and be a part of the team of thirty-three authors who co-authored the *13 Steps to Riches* series. My hunch from the very beginning was that this was outside my comfort zone, but I was curious and inspired by those who stood with me, shoulder to shoulder. I am honored and grateful for the opportunity as I continue to learn what it means to be a part of a team, and I am excited about where this journey will take me next.

Mastering all thirteen distinctions of the *Think and Grow Rich* book by Napoleon Hill has brought many emotions forward and forced me to really dig deep about how each intertwines with one another. Without Desire, Faith, Auto-Suggestion, Specialized Knowledge, Imagination, Organized Planning, Decision, Persistence, the Power of the Master Mind, Transmutation, and the Subconscious Mind, we may never achieve our Dream/Vision.

So, take this moment and realize that there are two paths you can take. You either take the road to poverty or to riches. Which do you choose? The road map and filling the tank to full is yours to make and no one else. There is no right/wrong, good/bad, blame/shame, or fault/guilt. The responsibility to choose is yours and yours alone. Thus, no excuse, judgment, assumption, or justification can be used to save you from accepting the responsibility if you either fail or deny the riches that life has to offer you, as acceptance relies on each of us controlling the one thing we can—our mindset.

As this journey ends, I will continue to be the inspiration, blossoming from surviving to thriving and beyond! This is my life's chosen path, and I choose to inspire others as I am inspired by those who come before me. I will continue to exercise my mind and trust my instinct so that my sixth sense is always focusing on the positive ways a human can be and interact with others.

As my dear friend Ruth Trembly so poignantly shared, we all have a responsibility to create the Quilt of Humanity from our own experiences and perspectives. This shall be mine. As I always share powerful quotes with you, this chapter will not be different than the prior ones.

"There is a Universal, Intelligent, Life Force that exists within everyone and everything. It resides within each one of us as a deep wisdom, an inner knowing. We can access this wonderful Source of Knowledge and wisdom through our intuition, an inner sense that tells us what feels right and true for us at any given moment."
~ Shakti Gawain

"Follow your instincts. That's where true wisdom manifests itself."
~ Oprah Winfrey

"Intuition is essentially the voice of grace, something that needs to be experienced to be understood and known. It has the power to open the passageway to inner illumination."
~ Unknown

"Inspiration is the whisper of the soul."
~ Jiddu Krishnamurti

It has been a true gift to be on this journey with all of you and follow your sixth sense and trust that when you feed your subconscious mind with positive and nurturing thoughts, the best is yet to come.

ELAINE SUGIMURA

About Elaine R. Sugimura: Elaine is an accomplished CEO turned Business Consultant / Life Strategist who has a passion to create Leaders amongst Leaders. With over thirty-five-plus years in the fashion and food and beverage industry, she has a passion to not only lead but support those who are seeking to reinvent who they are no matter where they are in life. She is a two-time breast cancer survivor and she knows a thing or two about surviving to thriving.

Fun fact: She is an adrenaline junkie—the higher, the faster, the better. Her love for adventure has led her to travel to many parts of the world by plane, train and automobile. She and her husband, Hiro, share their home in Northern California. They have raised two extraordinary sons, Bryce and Cole and have added two beautiful daughters-in-law, Erica and Giselle, to their growing family. Her legacy is to share what is possible when we open ourselves up to the issues that hold us back. Her life's mission is to move those who are just surviving into Thrivers!

Author's Website: *www.ElaineRSugimura.com*

Book Series Website: *www.The13StepstoRiches.com*

Elizabeth Anne Walker

MANY SEEK THEM BUT FEW FIND THEM

Proprioception, enteroception, faith, intuition, Divine guidance, elemental guidance, and gut feeling are all things that are referred to as the sixth sense. They are intangible to some and undeniably real to others. Many people seek them, and few find them in a way they are able to utilize them. People debate their validity and existence, and all successful people mention that they play a part in decision-making and staying ahead of the crowd. They lead to fast decisions, going against the grain, new inventions, new ways of doing things, adaptability, and innovation. They are also the one true warning system that successful people utilize.

So, how do you experience them? Some experience them via the elements, water, wind, fire, earth and Ether. Some through a feeling in their body, a knowing. Some via signs and symbols. Some by connecting to a God or their Guides. Some via ritual and dedication. Some via pure imagination. Some via faith in themselves and their abilities.

Those without them seek them and long for them, engaging hours and large amounts of finance in the pursuit of this connection via church services, tarot card readings, clairvoyants, spiritual healers, faith healers, miracle nights, intuition courses, galactic mind melds, spiritual nights, plant medicine, psychedelics, prayer, light language, extreme physical pursuits, and many more.

In fact, the global intuition industry is estimated to be worth over $200 billion and growing rapidly. The psychic industry in the USA alone is worth over $3 billion. Religious tourism in India is worth over $30 billion!

Those with it seem to easily create ideas, pivot easily in times of change, create successful inventions and innovations, build effective relationships, and seem to have it all. They seem to be successful in relationships both personally and professionally. They have financial and societal wealth and abundance. They have time—they do so much, yet they still seem to have time. They are relatively healthy and seem to experience abundant health when there is any infectious disease around them. Their careers and businesses seem to go from strength to strength, and they just appear to have it all!

Those who seek it often pay those who have it to learn it, and some learn it and become embodied in it and, therefore, start to utilize it and have it! And an interesting thing happens to those that don't. They often turn against the person they paid in an effort to destroy them. They feel the one they have paid has betrayed them because they didn't get what they wanted. The person providing the information gave it all to them, and deep down, they know it as if others were successful. Despite this, someone has to be blamed, so they continue to destroy themselves and their hope of gaining this sixth sense through slander and avoidance.

This betrayal of self and attempted destruction of others moves them further and further away from what they say they want. The sixth sense is only available to those who are willing to see themselves, examine themselves deeply, and accept responsibility for themselves in all they think, see, and act.

Those they paid to learn it from taught them well. They just didn't do it! They believed it was too simple. They were after the step-by-step guide and, despite being given it, thought that it all ended in the training.

Really, everyone has it; you just need to learn to access it. Once you access it, you will be compelled to perform a set of actions and circumstances with precision and dedication, tenacity and devotion, pertinacity and commitment. Those who embodied this and kept going developed it, and those who did not fell behind and eventually convinced themselves that it wasn't them. They returned to the delusion that they had little or no control of their world, particularly not over their fate as they moved through life.

So, if so many people want it, why do so few have it? And what is the secret that those who have it are keeping? Well, there is no big secret. In fact, successful people tell the secret all the time. And the seekers refuse to believe it. It's just too simple....

Firstly, imagine who you want to be. Imagine it and create it into a vision that is easy to bring to mind. Perhaps it's you speaking on a stage with people you look up to. Perhaps it is holding your newborn child. Perhaps it's driving the car of your dreams. Perhaps it's the way you see the world. Perhaps it's to heal your mind, body, or spirit. Whatever it is, create the vision in your mind and allow this vision to develop.

Seek imaginary and real counsel to develop the vision further so it becomes the only thing you focus on. By imaginary counsel, I mean use your imagination and, in your mind, ask these people what they would do next. You know more about others than you realize, and you can access all they know and their character right in your own imagination. Change the things they advise you to change and create all they advise you to create to achieve your imagination vision.

Make the vision really big and bright and tell everyone about it. It's okay if you change your mind later no one of any importance will mind. Make the vision at the forefront of all your thoughts, words, and deeds, and hold it there for the world to see. Become fully associated with your vision and the outcomes it will create.

Secondly, really feel it. What will it feel like in your body to be living your vision? What will you do differently? Start doing that now. What emotions will be primary for you? Start feeling them now. What music do you listen to? Start listening to it now. Who will you hang around with? Start hanging around them now, even if that means only via their podcasts or videos, still start. What will you eat? Start eating like that now. What about your health? Do the things now!

The embodiment of the sixth sense or intuition is often referred to as The Door to the Temple of Wisdom or the ticket to the new table. The golden tablet, the art of knowing. And it is only through dedicated practice that one will experience this themselves.

The years of hoping, wishing, and waiting will never match the acts of those in the doing. The fog of deception lifts when one fully embraces their mission and commits to it in a way only very few do. Prior to that, intuition will be sold as a simple gut feeling, which is usually dictated by fear. People say things like yes, I'm in, and not right now, my intuition is telling me to wait. That's fear in the body and mind.

True intuition is a decision able to be made with no second guessing. It's a knowing without knowing. And then the action that comes from that. The mere definition of intuition is to make sense of something without the need for justification or conscious reasoning.

Thirdly, act! Every single action you take must lead to your imagination's outcome in every single way! It's this that trips people up. This is where they get stuck. This is where they are unwilling to make the commitment to truly make use of the sixth sense. This is where they stop, usually just prior to intuition truly kicking in for the first time. Everything that moves you away from your imagined outcome MUST be eliminated. It can no longer exist. All commitment must be towards what you desire.

This is the piece that becomes unbearable for many. Having to deny friends and family access while you focus on your goal is often too much. Yet, it is in this quiet action that intuition tells us that we are on the right path. It starts to speak to you, guiding you on the way, warning you of pitfalls, and leading you the way you choose to be led. It is here that trust in self is built, and trust in the mission is built.

As this builds and builds, decision-making becomes easy as you have a deep internal knowing that your decisions are valid, and it's all completely inexplicable to others how you always manage to be in the right place at the right time.

You see, even reading this, you'll say it's too simple. The answers are always hidden in plain sight. Trust me, successful people know that this is everything, yet it seems too simple. That's why we say success is easy. That's why we say follow your heart and act. These things lead to you eventually taking action and being able to access intuition/sixth sense to give you an advantage over your own life's trajectory.

We are excited for the day you do that as we will celebrate you every step of the way, especially when you feel alone. We know we've been there, and we cannot wait to meet you in your glory!

ELIZABETH ANNE WALKER

About Elizabeth Walker: Elizabeth is Australia's leading Female Integrated NLP Trainer, an international speaker with Real Success, and the host of Success Resources (Australia's largest and most successful events promoter, including speakers such as Tony Robbins and Sir Richard Branson) inaugural Australian Women's Program "The Seed." Elizabeth has guided many people to achieve complete personal breakthroughs and phenomenal personal and business growth. With over twenty-five years of experience transforming the lives of hundreds of thousands of people, Elizabeth's goal is to assist leaders to create the reality they choose to live, impacting millions on a global scale.

A thought leader who has worked alongside people like Gary Vaynerchuck, Kerwin Rae, Jeffery Slayter, and Kate Gray, Elizabeth has an outstanding method of delivering heart with business.

As a former lecturer in medicine at the University of Sydney and lecturer in nursing at Western Sydney University, Elizabeth was instrumental in the research and development of the stillbirth and neonatal death pathways, ensuring each family in Australia went home knowing what happened to their child, and felt understood, heard, and seen.

A former Australian Champion in Trampolining and Australian Dance sport, Elizabeth has always been passionate about the mindset and skills required to create the results you are seeking.

Author's Website: *www.ElizabethAnneWalker.com*

Book Series Website: *www.The13StepsToRiches.com*

Erin Ley

YOUR BRIGHTEST ADVISOR

In *Think and Grow Rich,* Napoleon Hill refers to the Sixth Sense as "the door to the temple of wisdom opened by our Guardian Angel."

When I was in my hospital room at Memorial Sloan Kettering Cancer Center at age twenty-five, newly diagnosed with a rare, lethal form of cancer called non-Hodgkins lymphoblastic lymphoma, I discovered how important our sixth sense really is. Before this diagnosis, I left everything to chance. I believed everyone else knew what was best for me.

I didn't trust myself and my decisions until June of 1991, when I took my life back. I took my personal power back and began listening to my sixth sense. Most of us forget about that significant part of ourselves once we begin to take on the beliefs of others. We give more credibility to others' beliefs, opinions, and feelings regarding how we should live, thereby distancing ourselves from who we truly are.

The Sixth Sense is our guidance system informing us if we are on track or off track. Inspiration comes in ideas or simple hunches felt, moving us toward our desired goal or away from danger. I've learned that I compromised myself when I didn't listen to my sixth sense.

As a young girl, I learned not to trust my sixth sense. I am a Pisces, Empath, Clairsentient. I feel things very strongly. As a young girl, I felt things would happen before they did. When I was fourteen years old, my mother had me speak with a priest about this, and the priest told me what I felt was not a good thing and not a good path to take. So, I became frightened by my gift. I wanted nothing to do with it and buried it so deep that I forgot it was there. My feelings eventually caused me anxiety. Once I was diagnosed with cancer at age twenty-five, I learned that my gift was there to help not just me but others as well. I embraced it once again, regardless of what others thought, and it was lifesaving.

There were certain times during my protocol when I felt I would not be able to tolerate the chemotherapy, and I vocalized my concern. After pushback, the medical team adhered to my wishes of postponement, only to find out that my blood count was dangerously low and the chemotherapy could have killed me. I became my own biggest advocate, and my sixth sense became my brightest advisor.

In *Think and Grow Rich*, Napoleon Hill states that "somewhere in the cell structure of the brain, an organ receives vibrations of thought, which is ordinarily called "hunches." So far, science has not discovered where this organ of the sixth sense is located, but this is not important. The fact remains that human beings do receive accurate knowledge, through sources other than the physical senses. Such knowledge, generally, is received when the mind is under the influence of extraordinary stimulation."

We have the same power within each of us as that which creates worlds, keeps everything in orbit, and shares with us the beauty of Nature. Once we tap into this power, and we go from knowing it to being it, life opens in ways that many people refer to as miraculous.

Once I remembered this power within, my whole life began to transform. It was from the hospital bed in 1991 that I began craving personal development books. I studied Jon Kabat-Zinn, Shakti Gawain, Ester and Jerry Hicks, Neville Goddard, Norman Vincent Peele, Wayne Dyer, Bob Proctor, Napoleon Hill, and so many others who spoke about this incredible power and taught people how to access it. At the time, my intuition told me to begin teaching this to others, and that's what I was determined to go on and do. Teaching this became my white-hot burning desire.

I began teaching this to cancer patients when the doctors at Memorial Sloan Kettering Cancer Center started having their patients call me at home in the 1990s. They couldn't explain what I was doing. And that's when my Life Coaching career started.

Napoleon Hill refers to The Six Ghosts of Fear: poverty, criticism, ill health, loss of love of someone, old age, and death. In all of what I experienced, my sixth sense led me out of the fear and into exactly where I belong, living my best life. Here is where my sixth sense played a role in each:

1. **Fear of Poverty:** After the divorce was final in 2014, I became a single mom with three children, ages ten, eleven, and fifteen at that time. I stopped my Life Coaching business to focus on my family, and I believed the child support would come on time. It didn't. One night, I was in the supermarket with my daughter, and only five dollars, hoping it would be enough for the milk and bread I needed for my children. I was living with the fear of poverty until that moment.

   From that experience, I walked out of the supermarket, not the same woman who entered just twenty minutes before. I became inspired, and I understood the Law of Focus. My main focus then was to grow my business to six figures. I accomplished that in a year and a half. My business continues to grow year after year, and my children will always be my priority.

2. **Fear of Criticism:** There is a difference between constructive criticism and derogatory criticism. Constructive criticism is welcomed. My fear of derogatory criticism began when I was five years old. I had a Kindergarten teacher who was verbally abusive and very critical. My first-grade teacher continued with physical abuse and even more criticism.

   My fear of criticism was so bad that I wrote twenty-five-page papers in college in lieu of a three-minute speech—my fear of criticism ended at age twenty-five when I was living with a life-threatening cancer. My intuition kicked in, informing me that no one on this planet is any better or worse than another, no matter who it is, as long as they follow the Golden Rule. Since 1991, the negative opinions of others have meant nothing to me. I might become disappointed in someone I cared about if they criticized me; nonetheless, the opinion has zero impact on my life.

3. **Fear of Ill Health:** As you now know, I've overcome a form of cancer that very few survived in 1991. I know what I can do for myself and the healing powers I have within through Spiritual Universal Law, meditation, visualization, and affirmation. My sixth sense never allows fear of ill health.

4. **Fear of Loss of Love of Someone:** I went through a tumultuous divorce after being with my ex-husband for twenty-two years. At the end of the marriage, I had the fear of losing him. During the divorce, I was shocked and heartbroken. Once again, my intuition kicked in and began to lead me down the path to now living my best life. I listen to my gut, my instincts. On the other hand, when it comes to losing a loved one who has passed on, I know they are in a better place. Of course, I never want them to go, and I want to continue to feel their physical presence; however, I do believe they've passed on to Heaven, where we will meet again.

5. **Fear of Old Age:** I have no fear. What's the point of living in fear and wasting precious time? I take age one day at a time and I truly expect everything will work out exactly as it should. The older I get, the better life gets, and the wisdom compared to youth is immeasurable.

6. **Fear of Death:** After confronting the Grim Reaper in 1991, I refuse to make time for any kind of fear, especially death.

When we experience any kind of fear, please remember it is a dream crusher. Living life in fear, self-doubt, or worry will only attract us more of what we fear or worry about. To stop that momentum, the key is to fully focus on the things in life you are grateful for. Have faith that inspired ideas will come and provide the solution to every problem.

When we're in fear we don't think clearly. We cannot see the opportunities that are trying to show themselves to us. Quiet your mind and drop into your heart. Your sixth sense is your biggest ally and will never let you down. It's when we don't listen to it that things go wrong.

If you want to know more about how you can go from feeling stuck, overwhelmed, or distracted to becoming focused, fearless, and excited about life, I'd love to speak with you. As a Life Coach and Business Strategist, I love helping my clients live their best life. And I want that for you. Always remember to live onward and upward!

ERIN LEY

About Erin Ley: As Founder and CEO of Onward Productions, Inc., Erin Ley has spent the last thirty years as an Author, Professional Speaker, Personal and Professional Empowerment, and Success Coach predominantly around mindset, vision, and decision. Founder of many influential summits, including "Life On Track," Erin is also the host of the upcoming online streaming T.V. show, "Life On Track with Erin Ley," which is all about helping you get into the driver's seat of your own life.

People call Erin "The Miracle Maker!" As a cancer survivor at age twenty-five, single mom of three at age forty-seven, successful Entrepreneur at age fifty, Erin has shown thousands upon thousands across the globe how to become victorious by being focused, fearless, and excited about life and your future! Erin says, "Celebrate life and you'll have a life worth celebrating!"

To see more about Erin and the release of her fourth book, "WorkLuv: A Love Story," along with her "Life On Track" Course and Coaching Programs, please visit her website.

Author's Website: *www.ErinLey.com*

Book Series Website: *www.The13StepsToRiches.com*

Fatima Hurd

EMBRACING OPPORTUNITY

"Through the aid of the sixth sense, you will be warned of impending dangers in time to avoid them, and notified of opportunities in time to embrace them."
~ **Napoleon Hill**

Napoleon Hill best describes the Sixth Sense in this quote. For most of my life, I had a strong intuition about avoiding danger or embracing opportunity.

Although I did not know it then, I was very dependent on my intuition when I was younger. I always showed up at the right time and place, and opportunity would also show up. I mentioned this in one of the earlier chapters when I decided to go in person and submit an application at Caesar's Palace, where I intended to apply for one position that had already been filled at the time I showed up.

However, the right position opened up for me and led me to the position that was truly intended for me. It also opened up an opportunity that had a significant impact on the person I am today. That little voice we all have in us offers information that we selectively choose to act on or not. How we choose determines the consequences and effects it has on us physically and mentally.

As I have matured, my intuition has become more powerful, especially when I take action. I am also more in tune with the signs my body gives me when I am or am not in alignment with my intuition.

When I fail to listen or take action based on my intuition, I feel in my body first. If it's not in alignment with my body, I feel like I have a hole in my stomach and pressure in my chest, then I am stricken with an overwhelming feeling of anxiety, and my arms become tingly. I feel my body stiffen so tight that the next day, my body feels like I was struck by a truck. So, I've learned to trust and follow my intuition no matter how weird it sounds.

My intuition became more intense when I became a Reiki Master. It is so intense that I never question it, especially when I conduct sessions. As a Reik, I run my hands over a person's body, and I begin to receive specific information from that person's energy.

I believe that our intuition is meant to help guide us. As we develop this gift of "trusting the knowing," we no longer question what needs to be done. Our intuition is meant for much more than avoiding danger or embracing opportunities. It is meant to help us have a greater impact on the lives of others.

My life has been a long learning curve; I began my spiritual healing journey when I was sixteen. I became a certified Reiki Master to help heal myself. Honestly, I was ready to settle to just be Reiki certified for Level 1, which is to do healing for myself. However, my Reiki teacher encouraged me to become Reiki Certified as a Reiki Master, so I did it.

At that time, I didn't know yet, but I know now that her encouragement was no coincidence; it put me on the path of being able to create an impact in the lives of others. Thinking of staying level 1 was pretty selfish thinking on my part—all I could think of was healing myself, but my intuition knew better, and me saying yes to my teacher was not our blue. It was my being at the right place with the right teacher that led to me saying yes.

Later, I found out how my acceptance of becoming a Reiki Master truly created an impact in the lives of others. One experience in particular was with my best friend, Lisa. I met her one day when I walked into her classroom, and she gave me a slip of paper with the names and schedules of the students I was supposed to help. I was scheduled to sub all week.

At the end of the week, I remember her walking up to me with her big smile, giving me a big hug, and thanking me for helping out. She then asked me if I'd be interested in staying long-term. I meant to say no because, at the time, I had other plans, but instantly, my intuition and everything inside me refused to allow me to say no, and instead, I said yes. What? Why?

She was ecstatic and ran off to let the principal know before I could say anything else. I remember going home and trying to figure out every way to get myself out of the situation, but the more I thought about it, the more it just seemed to align with me. The schedule was perfect; it worked by allowing me to drop off and pick up the kids. So, I went with it.

Later on, after working with her not just at school but outside and doing Reiki sessions, she began to open up about so much and expressed her gratitude to me for receiving Reiki and how it transformed her life. This impact allowed her to show up for kids that she taught without the feeling of burnout that plagued her for years prior to her reiki session.

The dread that she used to feel before the start of the school year has transformed into joy, and she uses her tools to help bring peaceful energy into her classroom that supports her students to feel safe and engaged during their time in her classroom.

When I followed my intuition, I never imagined that my decision would have a greater impact than those right in front of me. It has spread because it has allowed her to create a huge impact on the lives of her students every year. Every year, her students move on to high school feeling empowered, supported, and, more importantly, enough because of the impact she causes in their lives before taking the bigger leap into high school.

Our intuition is much more than just navigation through life in alignment with right or wrong; when mastered, it becomes powerful enough to create impact and a ripple effect on all who come in contact with you.

Taking action and building up your intuitive muscle is a service to humanity because it stops being about us and becomes about how we can be of service. Once we have mastered that, life becomes so much more fluid that we don't need to try to be everything we think we need to be.

FATIMA HURD

About Fatima Hurd: Fatima is a personal brand photographer and was featured in the special edition of Beauty & Lifestyle's mommy magazine.

Fatima specializes in personal branding photographs dedicated to helping influencers and entrepreneurs expand their reach online with strategic, creative, inspiring, and visual content. Owner of a digital consulting agency, Social Branding Digital Solutions, Fatima helps professionals with all their digital needs.

Fatima holds ten years of photography experience. An expert in her field, she hosts workshops to teach anyone who wants to learn how to use and improve their skills with DSLR and in manual mode.

Hurd is also a mother of three, wife, certified Reiki master, and certified crystal healer. She loves being out in nature, enjoys taking road trips with her family, and loves meditation and yoga on the beach.

Author's Website: *www.FatimaHurd.com*

Book Series Website: *www.The13StepsToRiches.com*

Frankie Fegurgur

TRUSTING THE UNSEEN

In this final volume of *The 13 Steps to Riches*, we reach the culminating principle: The Sixth Sense. This step exceeds logic, diving into intuition, that inner compass is guiding us beyond reason to our most profound self. For me, intuition is not merely a reaction; it's tapping into a unique genius within each of us, something special that's uncovered when we close our eyes, become still, and silence the noise around us. In that quiet space, we hear a voice—a connection to our inner knowing.

Intuition and flow are intertwined; to tap into our inner genius, we must get into a state where things move seamlessly, like a meditative flow throughout the day. This state doesn't mean being oblivious but rather seeing things with fresh eyes, like a tourist in your own town. There's immense beauty in this perspective—commutes become a time to decompress, daily routines hold surprises, and life is no longer a grind but a journey of discovery.

When I encounter people who lack this genius flow, burdened by fear and struggling, I suggest starting with small promises to themselves. These small acts build self-trust. We're often taught to distrust our intuition, but I believe intuition is the feedback we receive when we enter a room, meet someone, or face a decision. Yet, fear keeps many from acting on that feedback. Fear seeps into the body, dictating actions and trapping us in cycles of anxiety. Learning to zoom out, stepping outside our current mindset, allows us to see that we don't have to figure it all out alone. A great coach or mentor isn't there to provide answers but to help you realize where you are and where you're going.

In my time with the Marines, we used land navigation, which involved orienting ourselves using a compass, the map, and even the sun's position. Nowadays, we rely so heavily on GPS to guide us, but there's an internal navigation system within us. Just like land navigation, to find our path, we must first know where we stand. This self-trust, built from small promises, enables us to walk with confidence rather than hunched over and disconnected from our own spirit.

There's power in recognizing when we're out of flow and taking steps to get back. Recently, I found myself frustrated with technology that wasn't syncing, causing my productivity to grind to a halt. I realized how much I was relying on those tools and had to ask myself: what can I do right now, despite these setbacks? I called someone I hadn't spoken to in a while and found that reconnecting re-energized me. It's about stepping outside yourself, finding what's exciting even when you're frustrated, and knowing that the next smallest step is enough.

We must each develop our own motto or mantra—a principle we can return to when the going gets tough. Mine is simple: put yourself in the best position to win daily. Success starts with showing up for yourself and being your biggest fan. Often, people think no one cares, but that's not the point; you're showing up for something larger than applause. Winning, for me, isn't about the accolades or the material gain; it's about the impact on those around me and the kind of person I become through the journey.

When we let go of fear and trust that voice within, we unlock our full potential. This journey isn't just about accomplishments but about embracing and navigating the unknown. Letting go is like standing on the edge of a cliff—terrifying but liberating. And clearing out mental clutter allows us to see the beauty in our surroundings and reconnect with our sense of purpose.

Each step builds toward something: a life where we're unbound by fear and attuned to the infinite possibilities within us. I hope readers take each step to heart and be open to intuition, even if it initially feels uncomfortable. Winning doesn't mean taking the same path as everyone else but finding the way that's meant for you.

I'd like to finish with a story that was pivotal in my journey, one that embodies trusting intuition over expectation. At seventeen, I was on track for a full scholarship to college—a dream for my working-class family. But one day, after school, I found myself at a friend's house, where I met a Marine recruiter. I was captivated by his presence, his commitment, and the challenge he presented. Without knowing exactly why, I signed the enlistment contract before my friends even did. My family was disappointed; they saw college as my way out of a hard life. But my intuition knew otherwise.

Joining the Marines, I found an education unlike any classroom could offer. Eight weeks into boot camp, 9/11 happened. Suddenly, the gravity of that day made me realize that I had made the right decision. Despite the hardships, I knew I was on the right path, and I became the first in my family to graduate from college afterward. That moment changed everything because I chose to follow my gut, even against well-meaning advice.

The sixth sense is about trusting that instinct, honoring it, and realizing that it's our ultimate guide. In serving this purpose, I've discovered that true leadership is about empowering others and believing in something larger than ourselves.

As we reach this final chapter in *The 13 Steps to Riches*, I leave you with this: Embrace your intuition and trust it deeply. When we do, life expands, and our path reveals itself in extraordinary ways.

FRANKIE FEGURGUR

About Frankie Fegurgur: Frankie's "burning desire" is helping people retire with dignity. Frankie distills the lessons he has learned over the last fifteen years and empowers our youth to make better financial decisions than the generation before them.

This is a deeply personal mission for him—he was born to high-school-aged parents, and money was always a struggle. Frankie learned that hard work alone wasn't the key to financial freedom and sought a more fulfilling path. Now, he serves as the COO of a nonprofit financial association based in the San Francisco Bay Area, teaching money mindfulness. He, his wife, and their two children can be found exploring, volunteering, and building throughout their community.

Author's Website: *www.FrankMoneyTalk.com*

Book Series Website: *www.The13StepsToRiches.com*

Fred Moskowitz

THE POWER OF INTUITION & STRATEGIES FOR DEEPER LISTENING

Intuition is something that inherently exists inside of us. We do not need to develop it because it is and always has been there. Learning to listen to our intuition is a capability that we work on and develop over time. And the more we listen to the lessons from our intuition, the better we become at hearing what it has to share with us.

Intuition is known by various names: hunches, whispers, and gut feelings. It is the sensation that you feel when answers and solutions suddenly inexplicably come to you. It may present itself as a strong feeling for not moving ahead with something or an impulse to choose one or another option when presented with multiple choices. It also can be the feeling of moving forward and accepting an opportunity or strong caution to exit a situation that does not seem right.

Learning to listen to our intuition is a skill that is developed and improves over time, much like how we develop our muscles when we exercise at the gym regularly. For myself, as a part of working on this skill, I like to spend time getting into the feeling of curiosity. If you feel a strong urge to do something or to move away from it, try following that urge and see what happens as a result. If you suddenly find yourself thinking about an old friend or colleague that you have not talked to in a while, give them a call and see what develops from the conversation.

Once you begin to experience positive outcomes from listening carefully to your intuition, it will start to reinforce your level of trust in your intuition and in the decisions that you make based on those feelings.

How can we take some actionable steps to start building and nurturing this skill? I find it helpful to start by observing reactions to events and occurrences throughout your daily life and noticing the feelings in your body.

Observe your physiological response to things that happen to you. Take a moment to scan your body for any tightness or other feelings of tension. Acknowledge and notice any of these feelings and the location of them in your body, such as in your stomach, chest, or neck. If you feel any uncomfortable physical feelings when you are faced with making a decision, pay very close attention because it could be your intuition speaking to you.

Actionable Strategies

When it comes to intuition, here are some actionable strategies that I invite you to explore:

Sleep with a notepad and pen near you so that you can immediately write down any ideas that might come to you while you are sleeping. There is so much information that comes from our subconscious mind while we sleep. If we do not capture them right away upon waking up, they could be quickly forgotten.

Take time out and get out in nature. Be by yourself for a couple of hours, or even a full day or multiple days. Getting out in nature places you outside of your normal environment and creates a state change for you, which opens up mental space for you to think clearly and receive inspiration and messages from your intuition.

Participate in some creative activities such as writing, drawing, painting, or playing a musical instrument. These skills activate different areas of your brain and allow space for your intuition to speak up.

Take some chances on the feelings that you get! Try acting on thoughts that come to you. If you find this approach to be difficult or risky, I invite you to start out with some low-stakes items, watch for the results, and see where you go from there.

Benefits of Journaling

Studies have shown that brief sessions of journaling for just fifteen minutes a day, three to five times each week, can result in a significant improvement in physical and mental health. The reason is that this sets us up for getting into a mode of feeling good and it primes the pump for us getting in touch with our intuition.

Some of the top benefits are maintaining focus on goals and objectives, tracking of progress, increased self-confidence, engaging multiple senses and enhancing the brain-to-hand connection, and finding inspiration.

Are you new to journaling and not sure where to start? I like the idea of beginning with gratitude and making a list of all the positive things that you are thankful for from the day (or if you journal in the morning, then write about things from the previous day). Celebrating the good things that happen to us will always make us feel good and will set a positive tone for executing our tasks and activities.

Sharing a Personal Story

I would like to share a story about a recent encounter of my own involving my "sixth sense." Some time ago, I had been involved in conversations with a prospective client about entering into a business transaction. The conversations started off cordially, as expected, and the deal looked promising.

However, over the course of time, I began to get a sense that the client was in a hurry to get everything done, and also, I noticed that they were just a little too eager about moving forward with the transaction. They even had asked me to shortcut some of our standard processes and procedures in order to expedite things, which I politely declined.

All throughout our multiple conversations, the common thread of unexplained urgency and just too much eagerness to do a deal was present. I felt a very uneasy feeling in my stomach and tension in my chest. Despite the strong notion that something was wrong, I pushed ahead and went against my feelings. I then proceeded to accept money from the client.

Over the course of the next couple of days, I felt like I had a dark cloud looming over my head, a constant nagging reminder that something was off about this transaction. At first, I ignored the feeling. As time went on, the feeling seemed to get louder and louder, calling out to my attention that something was simply not right. I was even waking up in the middle of the night with this business deal on my mind.

After ruminating over this for a few days, I took action, picked up the phone, called the client, and asked them to meet me in person to discuss the next steps. They agreed, and when we met, I handed them a check, returned their money, and told them that there were no hard feelings. I explained that after further consideration, this was not going to be a good fit for us, and I wished them well. Yes, I gave back the money and walked away from the deal. In business, this is sometimes called "firing your customer."

Afterward, I decided to start to investigate the client deeper and perform more thorough due diligence. As I suspected, the more that I looked, the more that I found. I had discovered that there were some unethical financial dealings and fraud in their past, and I breathed a sigh of relief, knowing that I had just avoided what could have been a very bad situation.

The biggest learning lesson for me is that not every investment opportunity is right for every person, and not every customer is a good fit for your product or business. And I especially learned to have a high respect for my intuition and to listen to it carefully in the future.

Learning to listen and get in touch with our intuition is largely a "learning by doing" skill. Just like physical fitness, pursuing it with consistent activity will make it improve and be stronger. Spending time getting into a state of curiosity, taking up creative activities, and watching out for physical cues are all tactics and strategies that will help us improve our ability to trust and listen to our intuition.

In the long run, it will help us to make better and faster decisions, to have a stronger sense of confidence, and to take decisive action toward our goals and dreams with excellence and mastery.

FRED MOSKOWITZ

About Fred Moskowitz: Fred Moskowitz is a Bestselling Author, investment fund manager, and speaker who is on a personal mission to teach people about the power of investing in alternative asset classes, such as real estate and mortgage notes, showing them the way to diversify their capital into investments that are uncorrelated from Wall Street and the stock markets.

Through his body of work, he is teaching investors the strategies to build passive income and cash flow streams designed to flow into their bank accounts. He's a frequent event speaker and contributor to investment podcasts.

Fred is the author of *The Little Green Book of Note Investing: A Practical Guide For Getting Started With Investing In Mortgage Notes* and contributing author in *The Principles Of David And Goliath* and *The Book Of Influence.*

Author's Website: *www.FredMoskowitz.com*

Book Series Website: *www.The13StepsToRiches.com*

Gina Bacalski

USING OUR INTUITIVE BRAINS

The K-Pop supergroup and global sensation, BTS, is insanely talented, beautiful, hilarious and fun to watch do just about anything. If they've filmed it, chances are I, along with all the other eight million ARMY's (Fanbase name of BTS), have seen it. One of the things that ARMY's around the globe love to see is how the members of BTS interact with each other, on and off the stage. They really are more like brothers than band members.

They love spending time with each other as much as they love spending time performing for ARMY's. For our viewing pleasure, they have several shows that they film and release regularly. *RUN BTS* is a variety show where we get to watch BTS play games, do challenges, and complete quests with one another.

Bon Voyage follows the seven-member super group as they go on vacation to various locations around the world. They also have a series of Behind the Scenes documentaries (*Burn the Stage, Break the Silence, Beyond the Star, Bring the Soul*) where we get to watch BTS in their world stadium tours and what they are doing and places they go in the locations they hold concerts.

In all of this media we get to consume, one thing is made abundantly clear. BTS is connected by something stronger than love or music. Countless times, they finish each other's sentences, walk in sync, fold their arms, move chairs, and cross their legs at the same time as at least one or two other members. I have even seen two members of BTS, Namjoon and Jungkook, randomly start singing the same exact snippet of another artist's song at the exact same time, and in harmony (give it a Google if you're bored). It's gotten to the point where BTS have made a game out of it and several *RUN BTS* episodes now actively try to play some sort of telepathy game. And it works Every. Single. Time.

The point of all this, is this "brain thing" that Napoleon Hill is talking about is real and actually works.

In my own personal life, I have had countless experiences where, randomly, things suddenly appeared in my mind, and I have thought of a loved one or someone I feel a connection to, and upon further investigation, that loved one was experiencing the thing I "randomly" thought about.

Sometimes, my husband and I take our ability to "read" each other's minds for granted and get annoyed at each other when someone gets something wrong.

My husband and I re-read this chapter in *Think and Grow Rich* in preparation to write this book submission, and he came home from the gym confessing to me that for the first time in his entire life, the thought entered his mind that he wanted to get a tattoo. From a very young age, Jay rejected the idea or thought that he ever wanted a tattoo and even served in a special forces unit in the military but refused to get the squad tattoo that the rest of his team got because he was so sound in his convictions that tattoos weren't for him.

So, when he came home from the gym, he was puzzled as to why he suddenly had these thoughts. But upon further exploration, he was quite certain he had picked up the brain wavelength from fellow gym goers where tattoos are often on display and abundant.

Upon re-reading this chapter, I also remembered the comical scene in the very first *Ghostbusters* movie where Bill Murry's character is doing "telepathy" experiments. In the scene, he has two test subjects hooked up to an electric shock device. As he holds up a card with the back of the card to the test subjects, they must correctly guess the shape that's on the card or receive a mild shock from the device. One of the test subjects is a beautiful blonde female that Bill Murray's character is flirting with and skewing the results, and only the other test subject, who is male, is receiving any of the electric shocks, even though he was the only one correctly guessing the card shapes.

Besides the connection I have with my husband, the times that this phenomenon has made the biggest impact on me is when I am in dedicated and focused mastermind groups.

Just yesterday, my religious group had a mastermind discussion where a member of the group asked how to talk about her religious beliefs in God with friends or those around her that have left the faith or don't believe as she does, without offending them or feel like she was pressing her beliefs on them.

After a few moments of quiet while we contemplated her query, I offered this sentiment: I have put a lot of thought into my personal "brand," so to speak. There are things that I want everyone to know about me through interacting with me personally or with my social media presence. I want everyone to know I love Jesus, Jay, and BTS. In that order. And that I have a great sense of humor while living my positive, full, and wonderful life. Jesus is a huge part of my life and I talk about Him as quickly as I do BTS or Jay.

Another person in the group agreed with my statement and offered up that someone else's opinion or trigger is not your responsibility to dance around. As long as you are being kind and respectful, don't sensor yourself in talking with those around you with things that mean the most to you.

A few other people gave their thoughts on the idea as well, and the discussion was very successful. Even though the original query wasn't one I had myself, I gained a lot by listening to the collective mind around me.

My business partner and I have had countless sessions where we thought about a problem or concern on our own and within seconds of us sitting down together to talk about it, all the answers come spilling from our mouths, minds, and fingertips almost faster than we can speak or write them down.

Our business, 3DKDrama, where we invite women to come to Korea to have a KDrama experience, including your own personal male lead, started as just that. Come to Korea and have fun pretending to be in a KDrama. We'll film and photograph the interactions and experiences you have with your English-speaking male lead, and at the end, you get to go home with a KDrama that you were in! Sounds pretty cool, right? We thought so too. But there's more.

As we developed ideas and developed ourselves as leaders among women, we knew something major was missing from our big idea. As we thought about it further, and after many mastermind sessions on the topic, we concluded that not only did these wonderful women get to come and have an incredible experience in Korea with a beautiful male lead, but we wanted them to be able to go back to their homes knowing they were the female lead of their own lives.

Through more mastermind sessions, we developed a program of growth, love, and beauty for these women to grow and love themselves in ways they couldn't in any other construct. When they leave us, they will be empowered to do the things, and take the risks, and live the lives they only dreamed about, and they will have the tools to do so using their divine femininity.

We never would have come up with the program or even had the idea in the first place if we hadn't gotten together to mastermind about it. Now, when we are together, our minds are so connected that when we tap into "mind stimulation," we are an explosive force for good in the world. And I unabashedly and boldly write that statement and know that it's true in my heart and soul.

This is just a small part of what how using the subconscious mind and the creative imagination have done and are doing for me. I wonder what it will do for you!

GINA BACALSKI

About Gina Bacalski: Gina is a Real Estate Agent, licensed since June 2018. Her background is in Early Childhood Education where she received her Child Development Associate from the state of Utah and has an AS from BYU-Idaho. For the past seventeen years, Gina thoroughly enjoyed her experience in the service industry helping families in the gifted community.

In 2019, Gina helped Jon Kovach Jr. in his launch of Champion Circle. She brings her genuine love for people, high attention to detail, and strives to exceed client's expectations to the Real Estate industry.

Gina married the man of her dreams, Jay Bacalski, in San Diego, in 2013. The Bacalski's love entertaining friends and family, going on hikes, and attending movies and plays. When Gina isn't helping her clients navigate the real estate world, she will most often be found dancing and listening to BTS, watching KDramas and writing fantasy, sci-fi and romance novels.

Author's Website: *www.MyChampionCircle.com/Gina-Bacalski*

Book Series Website: *www.The13StepstoRiches.com*

Griselda Beck

TRUST YOURSELF: CALIBRATING YOUR INTUITION

The Sixth Sense is our intuition—our inner wisdom, knowing, truth, compass, and guide. It is also our energetic and cosmic connection to the Universe, God, Source, humanity, and life! Our intuition is our greatest resource, and yet so many of us are cut off or disconnected from it. Perhaps you feel it every now and then, but what if you could access it on demand whenever you needed or desired answers?

Breaking & Rebuilding Trust

First, let's get curious about how we go about disconnecting from our intuition in the first place. When we are born, we are highly instinctual. We feel something, and we cry. We don't think about it or weigh our options… we just go for it! Have you ever been around little kids when they are learning to express themselves and speak up for their needs? They are ruthless, honest, and direct with zero filter!

Somewhere along the way, we begin to give up a little power each time our voice gets shut down, either because we get something wrong, we get in trouble for something, or we're not able to do something. We lose a bit of self-trust through each of these events, which is replaced with feelings of self-doubt, not being good enough, and powerlessness. This creates a disconnection from our own wisdom as we begin to take in and rely on feedback from the outside world.

As we go through adolescence and well into adulthood, we break trust with ourselves in a million little (and a few BIG) ways every time we fall out of integrity with ourselves. Being out of integrity with ourselves can look like this:

- Not following through on something we said we would do
- Saying "yes" to things that we don't really want to do
- People pleasing
- Falling short or quitting on our own goals and dreams
- Putting others' needs above our own
- Putting the needs of our employers above our own
- Anytime you feel like you just "sold your soul to the devil"
- Anytime we harm ourselves (addictions or other self-harming acts)
- Not speaking up when you had something to say or were feeling some way

These are just a few common examples. That last one is a big one!

Think of a time that someone you cared about broke their word to you. They flaked and didn't come through. Something else was more important. How did you feel? How do you feel about going to them again and relying on them?

Let's take this into practice! Grab your journal or audio recording device… you may speak/record or write this down. I highly recommend writing if it is available to you, as it is more effective in processing and releasing.

Take that in for a minute. Close your eyes… yes, right here, right now.

Connect to the moment you realized they weren't coming. What emotions come up for you? Sadness? Disappointment? Anger? Resentment? Loss of Trust? Write for two to five minutes (or speak and record it).

Where do you feel that in your body? How does it feel in your body? Tightening of the chest? Anxiety feeling in the pit of your stomach? A pulsating or dull headache? Is your throat on fire? Write for two-five minutes (or speak and record it).

Name ten other times you have felt this exact same feeling. Recall the very first time you remember having this feeling. Write for two-five minutes (or speak and record it).

I use this exercise with my clients as a gauge of where to begin the inner work and where to go next. Through each event, we scan the mind, body, and soul (our soul is our energetic field and connection to the source) to identify the limiting beliefs that got recorded, what the underlying truths really are, feeling and releasing all that no longer serves.

We literally unblock the "stuckness" in their mind, body, and energy. This creates an abundant flow and opens up the manifestation channels, allowing what you desire to come into your life via infinite possibilities.

Now, with a clear and open channel, we can tune into our bodies and energy and tap into its infinite wisdom for powerful decision-making, grounded confidence, and speaking from authority.

Tapping into Our Sixth Sense

The practice of tapping into our intuition and, more importantly, trusting our intuition is truly just that, a practice. Our intuition and sixth sense is always activated and every single one of us has it. You may have heard of people called "intuitives," "mediums," and the like.

While there may be some people who misuse or misrepresent these special powers, they do actually exist. They are very real, and you also have that special power within you. We all do. The degree to which you can receive information (aka a transmission, download, message, etc.) is the degree to which you are attuned to it and you trust it.

Our bodies are always speaking to us, but most of us in the culture of "hustle," "busy," and "results" often do not pay attention or seek to listen and understand what it is conveying to us. We pop a pill for headaches or indigestion or numb out by having a drink, a drag, or a hit when we feel this discomfort.

Sometimes, our attachment to a specific outcome is so tight that we ignore these messages and focus on controlling our experience to "make it happen." Often in business, this approach works—to a limited extent, which we may not even be conscious of.

The challenge with this "forceful" approach is that it can often create disconnection with self and others, therefore damaging relationships and trust with ourselves and others. People may do what we want, but if they don't do so willingly, the resulting outcome is not as powerful *or* could be more temporary than we had hoped. Think about that difficult client, the partner that always results in conflict, the shame or disappointment time and time again that you feel.

This approach certainly doesn't work when it comes to creating a loving, deeply connected relationship, which is what most of us truly crave. Instead, it creates the opposite—disconnection, disappointment, mistrust, and resentment. Walking on eggshells and being on "probation" never feels good—in business or in life!

Leading our life, business, and relationships by listening to and trusting our "gut feeling" may sometimes lead to getting one wrong here and there, which is the price of a missed opportunity, but much more often than not, you win—and you WIN BIG! Those wins more than make up for those missed opportunities, and those missed opportunities actually become valuable lessons we carry forward and enrich our lives for the better.

Learning to trust ourselves and tune into our intuition is one of the most visible and frequently shared secrets to success that most people miss entirely or give up on.

But how? How do I practice? How do I access my intuition?

I'm glad you asked! It truly is a practice and can take some time, depending on your own journey tempo, openness, and willingness to "do the work." Here are some ways to begin and accelerate your practice.

- **Mindfulness:** According to Google, mindfulness is "a mental state achieved by focusing one's awareness on the present moment, while calmly acknowledging and accepting one's feelings, thoughts, and bodily sensations, used as a therapeutic technique." In short, mindfulness is about practicing being present. There is an abundance of mindfulness practices (both active and passive) you can try, such as meditation, breath work, coloring, tantra as a spiritual practice, driving, showering, etc. Notice where and when you get "ideas" while in these mindful activities.

- **Embodiment:** Moving your body increases blood flow and allows your body to release emotion (aka "stuck energy") by expending energy, sweat, and releasing waste. Ever notice the difference in how you feel before and after a walk in nature, a yoga or gym "sesh," post orgasm, dancing or singing, a massage or acupuncture, quality time with yourself or a loved one, etc.? There is a little zing of euphoria (or a big one), and you just "feel good."

- **Start Here:** If this is new to you, you can start by setting your alarm on your phone for five minutes (later, this will increase to ten, then twenty minutes and beyond). Meditate—simply sit or lay in stillness. If you have a thought come into your mind, notice it without judgment, resistance or pushing it away. If you feel the urge to fidget, scratch an itch, etc., simply notice it and try not to "do" anything about it; remain still.

If you start to feel anxious or any other emotion, notice it without judgment, trying to understand it or process it away… simply notice it. Once the alarm goes off, repeat the setting for five minutes and journal about your experience. What did you notice? What came up for you? Some things may be trivial. Some may reveal some wisdom. Do this practice daily for at least seven days. I usually have my clients do this for thirty days to start. It can take up to three weeks to really get the hang of it, for it to start to feel grounding vs weird, and for you to notice what is truly coming from it.

- **Hire a Coach:** There are many great books (such as this one), courses, masterminds and retreats you can read, take and join. Hiring a coach who is an expert in this field can support you in your journey and accelerate your results. They can help you identify your blind spots, navigate the journey of processing and releasing, stepping into your power, connecting to your body and truth.

Secret to Success

Most "millionaire secrets" type content out there has a huge emphasis on meditation and physical movement. It's not about being a Yogi or Gym Rat. It is not about spirituality or looks. It has everything to do with accessing your intuition because they know that the *real answers and success secrets come from within*. That is how trailblazers, innovators, and leaders create a path, doing what has not been done before—not just *following* others.

YOU are a leader! I know that because you are reading this right now. Create your own path, be your authentic self, and TRUST YOURSELF! There is always a bit of a learning curve to get the foundation of something new…, but at some point, you just need to turn off the noise and search within yourself for direction. Be still, listen, and trust.

Everything you need to have, everything you desire is truly INSIDE YOU!

GRISELDA BECK

About Griselda Beck: Griselda Beck, MBA, is a powerhouse motivational speaker and coach who combines her executive experience and expertise with transformational leadership, mindset, life coaching, and heart-centered divine feminine energy principles. Griselda empowers women across the globe to step into their power, authenticity, hearts, and sensuality, to create incredible success in their business and freedom in their lives. She creates confident CEOs.

Griselda's clients have experienced success in quitting their 9-5 jobs, tripling their rates, getting their first client, launching their first product, and growing their business in a way that allows them to live the lifestyle and freedom they want. She has been featured as a top expert on *FOX*, *ABC*, *NBC*, *CBS*, *MarketWatch*, *Telemundo*, and named on the Top 10 Business Coaches list by *Disrupt Magazine*.

Griselda is an executive with over fifteen years of corporate experience, founder of Latina Boss Coach and Beck Consulting Group, and serves as president for the nonprofit organization MANA de North County San Diego. She also volunteers her time teaching empowerment mindset at her local homeless shelter, Operation Hope-North County.

Author's Website: *www.LatinaBossCoach.com*

Book Series Website: *www.The13StepsToRiches.com*

Jeffrey Levine

THE SIXTH SENSE POWER

The Sixth Sense is defined as a way through which infinite intelligence may and will communicate voluntarily without any effort from, or demands by, the individual. It has been referred to as "the receiving set" through which ideas, plans, and thoughts flash into the mind. The flashes are sometimes called "hunches" or inspirations. Through the aid of your sixth sense, you will be warned of impending dangers in time to avoid them and notified of opportunities in time to embrace them. In this chapter, I will share some stories where my sixth sense had an impact on my life.

I awakened on Sunday of the last day of the month and saw a picture of a new Mercedes convertible in my mind. It was so clear and vivid that I didn't know what to make of it. I also felt a tug to get out of bed and quickly drive to the Mercedes dealership. Even though I would arrive thirty minutes before it opened, I quickly dressed and arrived before anyone else.

Quickly thereafter, several people lined up behind me. Since there was only one Mercedes convertible in the showroom, and I had arrived at the dealership first, I was the first to test drive it. As it was the last day of the month, the salesman offered me an unbelievable deal on the price of the car, providing me with a straightforward decision since the other people in line also wanted to test drive the car. Because of the tug to get out of bed and drive to the dealership, I had a brand-new car.

For many years, I owed money on a debt. Because the payment was rather large, it challenged my cash flow, creating a negative monthly balance. The pain occurred year after year. Eventually, it became very clear to me that the situation had to change. At that point, since I understood the laws of the universe, I turned it over to the higher laws, which would figure out how and send the answer my way.

A few months later, I received a letter from the bank stating my loan had been forgiven. Because I thought the letter was a mistake, I continued to pay on the loan, assuming it was my responsibility to do so. During that time, I was a member of a success club. I took a great training, which included reading books such as *Think and Grow Rich*, *The Magic of Believing*, and *The Magic of Thinking Big*.

I also listened to high-vibrational training, such as Brian Tracy and Wayne Dyer. I was also either reading books or listening to CDs on a daily basis, which relaxed me and raised my vibration. That eventually led me into a deep theta state where the magic occurred. A few weeks later, I received another letter from the bank stating there was no longer a loan and no further payments should be made.

When you live in the quantum world, do you understand that your job is not to figure out the how but rather the want of your dreams? Once you figure out what you want, you hand it over to the universe to figure out the how. This is when the magic happens.

I never expected my loan to disappear and be forgiven. Things like this have happened to me and blown my mind. The power of being in a quantum state can give you results that you could never have imagined. One morning at my local library, I read and studied the curriculum from *The Master Key System* by Charles F. Haanel.

After finishing my studies, I went to the gym, ran a couple of errands, and then went home. When I got home, I went to make a call and realized I didn't have my cell phone. I called the library (from my landline), and they said they would look for it, but they shortly called back and said my phone was not there. Since I had spent most of my day there, I went back and looked everywhere, but they were right: no phone. I continued to retrace my steps, but my phone was nowhere to be found.

A few hours later, I realized that I was trying too hard to find my cell phone. From reading and studying *The Master Key System*, I knew that this was not the right way to find my phone.

I let it go, sat down at my desk, and started reading my favorite books: *Think and Grow Rich* and *The Magic of Thinking Big*. By doing that, I became more relaxed, and the information in the books raised my vibration. Because I was reading and relaxing, I eventually went into a deep theta state, which relaxes the mind.

I kept receiving downloads that I should go to my computer. That didn't make sense at all, but I did it anyway. I went to the computer and found an app to find my phone, which hadn't been there before. All of a sudden, I saw a picture of my phone at the library. The app asked me if I wanted an alarm on my phone with a message giving a phone number to call.

All of a sudden, I received a phone call that my cell phone had been found in the library. I was told that a student sleeping near the phone was awakened by the alarm and quickly brought it to the front desk. The people at the front desk saw the message to call a certain number, and they did just that.

The odd thing is that the app I used to find my phone is nowhere to be found on my computer. This is the magic of the sixth sense.

My son had always been interested in going into my business and taking it over. For that reason, I never had to worry about transferring it to anyone else, and my business would stay in the family. But then he enrolled at Arizona State University and started talking about how beautiful the weather was and how much he liked it there.

As he spent more time in Arizona, he became noticeably less interested in returning to upstate New York to run my business. He finally told me that he was not going to return to New York to run my business. While I respected his decision, it presented me with a huge challenge: I was ready to move on from my New York business, but I had no one to sell it to.

Soon thereafter, a woman I didn't know approached me at the gym where I worked out every night. She introduced herself to me and said her partners were interested in buying my business when I was ready to sell. I did not know them, and I couldn't figure out how they knew that I wanted to sell the business. It was totally off the radar.

Since I was ready to sell, I decided to meet with them, and they offered me a price I couldn't refuse. Their offer was higher than I expected, and a lot more than I thought the business was worth. I said yes, sold my business, and was off to Arizona, where I would spend my winters enjoying the gorgeous weather.

The sale of my New York home is a perfect example of what happens when you stop trying to figure out how to make something happen but instead focus and allow your sixth sense power to provide the results. My New York property had been for sale for five years, but no one had looked at it or made an offer during that time.

While waiting for it to sell, I had been living in Arizona during the winter months and traveling back to New York, where I spent my summers. The trip from Arizona to New York was a long one, 2,500 miles, and with a brand new grandson in Arizona, I didn't want to be away in New York all summer.

When I was at my New York home that summer, I received a call from a prospective buyer who wanted to see the house. He was a challenge. Not only did he offer me a ridiculously low price, but he also wanted me to spend $10,000 or more to remove the underground oil tank. That did not work for me. He was not the right buyer.

A few days later, I heard a knock at the door. I don't usually receive unannounced visitors, so I was really surprised. The person said, "I was in the neighborhood just walking, and I wanted to know if your house is for sale. It looks so beautiful." I said, "Of course."

That person said he was renting and had just decided to take a walk up the road; he wasn't sure why. He looked at the property and loved it. He was just taking a walk and had no intention of buying a property.

That is how the power of the sixth sense works. Since I used it and had phenomenal results that would appear almost impossible to most people, you can use this power to provide yourself with some amazing results.

JEFFREY LEVINE

About Jeffrey Levine: Jeffrey is a highly skilled tax planner and business strategist, as well as a published author and sought-after speaker. He's been featured in national magazines, on the cover of *Influential People Magazine*, and is a frequent featured expert on radio, talk shows, and documentaries.

Jeffrey attended the prestigious Albany Academy for high school and then went on to the University of Hartford in Connecticut, the University of Mississippi Law School, and Boston University School of Law, and earned an L.L.M. in taxation. His accolades include features in *Kiplinger* and *Family Circle Magazine*, as well as a dedicated commentator for Channel 6 and 13 news shows, a contributor for the *Albany Business Review*, and an announcer for WGY Radio.

Jeffrey has accumulated more than thirty years of experience as a tax attorney and certified financial planner and has given in excess of 500 speeches nationally. Levine is the executive producer and cast member in the documentary *Beyond the Secret: The Awakening*.

Levine's most current work, *Consistent Profitable Growth Map*, is a step-by-step workbook outlining easy-to-follow steps to convert consistent revenue growth to any business platform.

Author's Website: www.*Strategies.org*

Book Series Website: *www.The13StepsToRiches.com*

Lacey & Adam Platt

NOT THE MOVIE & TRUSTING YOUR INTUITION TO ACHIEVE YOUR GOALS

Not the Movie

When people hear about the Sixth Sense, they immediately go to the movie and get creeped out. What I want to talk about goes beyond the movie.

Some people call it a gut feeling, an ah-ha moment, or a hunch. I call this inspiration my sixth sense. I know that I receive inspiration from multiple different directions. Sometimes it's a higher version of myself. Sometimes, it's those around me who have my best interest at heart, and sometimes, it's a higher power or angelic inspiration.

"The Sixth Sense is the medium of contact between the finite mind of man and infinite intelligence and for this reason it is a mixture of both the mental and the spiritual."
~ Napoleon Hill

There is no mistake in this principle being saved for last! You must first have an understanding of the previous steps before this one will make sense. Most people reject the idea of having a sixth sense because it sounds too woo-woo or unimaginable. To them I say, you must open up your mind in order to receive it. You can learn this through the practice of meditation or learning to just simply quiet your mind. Whatever it takes to slow down your brain and tune into something greater and higher than you. If you are open to this, then the world really starts to open up to you in ways it's never been able to before.

While writing this chapter it came to my attention that I have read this chapter of the book *Think and Grow Rich* only once before. For some reason, I would start the book over every single time I picked it up instead of picking up where I left off. Don't you think that's interesting? When you dive deep into a series of books or even just a single book with chapters that cause you to take action and really change, it takes time.

For me, I've always had a deep connection to spiritual things. Even though I was not raised in a very religious environment. I honestly believe that that helped me to really choose which way I wanted to go based on the experiences in my life. Through trial and error, I realized what it meant to feel the spirit with me versus not with me.

This principle of "The Sixth Sense" is one that I hold very closely to my heart. It is a side of myself that I have always been leery of sharing because there have been multiple times throughout my life when I've shared it and lost friends. It's very hard for most to understand. It requires digging deep within oneself to allow another source to help you with guidance and direction. Most people think, "I got this, I can do this. I don't need anybody else's help." But WOW, what are we missing out on if we have this type of attitude?

I want you to think about a time in your life when you followed a hunch, a gut feeling, or an idea that just kind of jumped into your head. Can you give it more power than just that? Can you realize that it's coming from a different source then you?

While rereading Napoleon Hills' chapter on "The Sixth Sense," I finally felt like I have someone who understands what I have gone through most of my life. I always felt like an outsider, someone who looked at the world differently and that nobody really understood. What I saw and felt has so much power! Reading someone else's words who has experiences like I do helps me to realize it's okay to be different! It's okay to experience the world differently than others, and even when you're told you're a freak or that you think too far outside the box, that just means it's more about that person who said it than it is about you! They are simply saying that they cannot comprehend how you do or know what you do, and that's okay!

Even though science cannot explain how the brain receives vibrations from the sixth sense, it doesn't really matter! Once you've experienced it, you're a believer. If you've never experienced a hunch, a gut feeling, or just a thought that you couldn't explain where it came from, it doesn't mean you can't. It just means you need to try to slow your mind down and be open to receiving information beyond your brain's capacity to come up with it.

In doing so, you *will* receive guidance and direction that will either help you avoid something bad or help you build something amazing! This I know from experience. Give it a try!

~ Lacey Platt

Trusting Your Intuition to Achieve Your Goals

A person's sixth sense is the key to achieving what you want in life. This sixth sense refers to one's intuition, that gut feeling that guides us toward the right decisions, the right opportunities, and ultimately towards wealth and success.

While some may dismiss intuition as a mystical or unscientific concept, the truth is that we all possess this innate ability to sense and interpret information beyond what our five senses can detect. This sixth sense is often the difference between those who achieve great success and those who struggle to make progress in their lives.

To develop our sixth sense, we must first learn to trust it. We must learn to listen to our gut feelings and act on them, even when they may seem illogical or risky. This requires a certain level of self-awareness and introspection, as we must learn to distinguish between our true intuition and our fears, biases, and past experiences.

One way to cultivate our intuition is through meditation and mindfulness practices. By quieting our minds and focusing on the present moment, we can become more attuned to our inner voice and the subtle signals that guide us toward our goals. We can also learn to recognize and release the negative thoughts and emotions that often cloud our judgment and prevent us from taking bold action.

Another key aspect of developing our sixth sense is to surround ourselves with positive influences and like-minded individuals. We become the sum of the people we associate with, so it is crucial to seek out mentors, coaches, and peers who support our vision and encourage us to take risks and pursue our dreams.

Of course, developing our intuition is not a one-time event but rather a lifelong journey. As we encounter new challenges and opportunities, we must continually tune in to our inner voice and adapt to changing circumstances. We must also learn to distinguish between our intuition and our ego, which may seek to lead us astray with false promises of fame or fortune.

Ultimately, the sixth sense is the key to achieving not just material wealth but also a sense of purpose, fulfillment, and happiness. By trusting our intuition and following our passions, we can create a life that is truly our own and inspire others to do the same.

I have used the ability to trust my sixth sense a number of times in my life. One such moment was when I wanted to quit my job to work on mine and my wife's business to help people achieve more. I was quitting a good, stable job with good pay, but I knew there was more out there for me to do, and I could feel it in my gut that I was meant for so much more.

I quit my job and we took our savings and some of the money out of my 401k to help supplement my income as we built the business. It was hard, and for a year, we struggled with how to make it work. We almost lost just about everything, and we really struggled financially.

Just as we had started to lose hope so many amazing opportunities just fell into our lap, and we have been able to build and work on the life we have always wanted. When you follow those intuitive moments, even if you can't see the full path forward, you will always see the rewards if you keep moving forward.

I couldn't be more grateful in my life for the struggle I have had to go through when I have done what I know I should do and listened to that gut feeling, that intuition. It's not always an easy path, but it's worth it.

In conclusion, the sixth sense is a powerful tool that we all possess but may not always trust or develop to its full potential. By cultivating our intuition through meditation, positive influences, and a willingness to take risks, we can unlock the key to achieving our dreams and creating a life of abundance and fulfillment.

As Napoleon Hill wrote, "Whatever the mind can conceive and believe, it can achieve," and our intuition is the guiding force that helps us bring those desires into reality. So, trust your gut, follow your heart, and let your sixth sense lead you towards what you truly desire.

~ Adam Platt

LACEY & ADAM PLATT

About Lacey Platt: Lacey is an energetic, fun-loving, super mom of five! She is an Achievement Coach, Speaker and new Bestselling Author who enjoys helping everyone she can by getting to know what their needs are and then loving on them in every way that she can. Her ripple effect and impact has touched the lives of so many and continues to reach more lives every single day. Allow Lacey to help you achieve your goals with proven techniques she has created and perfected over years of coaching. She and her husband have built an amazing coaching business called Arise to Connect serving people all around the world.

About Adam Platt: Adam is an Achievement Coach, Speaker, Trainer, Podcast Host and now a Bestselling Author. Adam loves to help people overcome the things stopping them from having the life they really want. Adam owns and operates Arise to Connect. Adam believes that connection with yourself, others, and your higher power are the keys to achievement and greater success in life. He is impacting thousands of people's lives with his message and coaching. He lives in Utah with his wife, five daughters, and dog, Max.

Author's Website: *www.AriseToConnect.com*

Book Series Website: *www.The13StepsToRiches.com*

Louisa Jovanovich

HARNESS YOUR INNER VOICE

Our intuition is often described as a gut feeling or internal voice that serves as an inner guidance system, helping us connect with our surroundings on a deeper level. It is an instinctive response to the world around us that functions outside of our conscious thought processes and enables us to perceive and experience things beyond our five senses.

Humans have sought to understand our senses and our interactions with the world and within ourselves since we first had thought. The most common framework is the five physical senses. Some speak of a sixth sense, a mysterious and unexplainable ability to perceive things beyond our five physical senses, while others brush it off as superstition or pseudoscience.

I personally believe this sixth sense is an innate ability we all possess. Recent studies have shown that our gut feelings are a real phenomenon that plays a significant role in our everyday decision-making processes, from simple tasks to life-changing situations.

Until the birth of my first child, I thought my natural instincts would be enough to raise a child. I believed I would instinctively know what they needed and how to take care of them without needing that knowledge. I soon came to find out, as does every parent, that is not the case, on many levels.

My gut told me this would not be as easy as just loving your child and giving them what they needed daily. I would go to sleep every night afraid that I was going to do a terrible job being a parent. I listened to everyone else tell me what I needed to do before I could even do it. This awareness gave me so much compassion towards my parents. I now look back at the way I was raised, and I no longer blame them for what I thought wasn't right.

In addition to my coaching business, I'm also a hairdresser. Being a hairdresser is a lot like being a coach... with scissors. I often share my feelings with my clients and listen to their stories and feelings. I learned long ago that I was not alone in my fears. Most of us felt like we were barely making it and always trying to keep our heads above water. And when you feel that way raising kids, it doesn't just impact your relationships with your children, but it also impacts your relationship with your significant other.

I had been watching my parents' relationship my entire life and judging it. I realized I had brought it into my own life. I had continued hoping it would just get easier, even as it continued to get worse. Everything I said I would never do, I was doing it. My dream of being a mother and wife was not as beautiful as I had created in my head. Nothing felt natural or easy for me.

I have had the privilege of being around some great minds collaborating. It's an interesting space to actually work backward, creating from the future backward. When we spend time worrying about the future, we are almost stepping unconsciously right into creating it. For example, my fear of who I was going to be as a mom and a wife. I had huge hopes I could be different from my fears. I could wish to do it right and succeed, but my fear of being like my parents and feeling not good enough had me step right into that space.

Most of us spend our time worrying about the future and regretting the past instead of being in the present moment where peace lives. Unknowingly, we are on the hamster wheel all day long, not even realizing that we are doing this. When we worry about the future, we feel fear and anxiety. When we worry about the past, we feel anger, regret, depression, guilt, or shame. Unknowingly, we then emote that out into the quantum zero-point field and attract situations, people, and circumstances that are also vibrating on that same low frequency and onto our bodies, where these negative emotions show up as injuries, dysfunctions, and illnesses.

So, healing involves changing my experience of who my parents were to what they should have been for me, and how they should have been with each other. It means changing my upsetting feelings about the past to one of having grace for who they are and living in gratitude for the love, compassion, and positive lessons they gave me. That opens up so much more space for love and growth.

When I'm coming from love, I'm in the present moment, where I am awake and living, creating and living the life I want. It gives me a sense of peace and satisfaction knowing I matter and knowing the experiences I have had get to be shared in the world to make a difference. When I see that in me, I see that in you.

We are here to truly see and experience our worth. I grew up very shy and very afraid of taking action. This work has given me the freedom to not live secretly being someone who sees what's possible and hopes she can make a difference, to being someone who is actually doing so.

My sixth sense began to adapt as I learned to trust myself and my own instincts, and I really started to understand and be present in what people needed from me. It was not to be told what to do and how to do it, but to communicate—talking and listening—in each situation. I have also used this space as a coach.

People I work with are not looking to be told what to do. They want to learn how I will guide them to uncover their own internal truth. I am able to help them do that in part because I have come to realize how insightful we all are. I was taught to follow the rules and do what I was told, which I did a terrible job of following, I may add. I found myself rebelling from rules and feeling controlled.

This made me feel like I was failing as a child. So how was I starting to follow this new path of the sixth sense in my adult life? Having learned that the 6th sense needs to be cultivated, I started working to improve it.

One way to develop our intuition is through meditation practices like mindfulness or journaling exercises, where you pay attention to your thoughts from a curious perspective and always without judgment. These techniques are a consistent practice in the eight-week course that I teach.

When we trust ourselves completely through our intuition, we tend to make decisions from a place of clarity and become significantly less stressed. Once you trust your instincts, you become less reliant on other people's opinions or information sources.

Moreover, tapping into this sixth sense enables us to make clear decisions and equips us with the power of creativity to open up limitless possibilities in thinking outside the box- where solutions may come from unconventional sources and solving problems might require an unconventional approach.

The idea of the sixth sense can be traced back to ancient times when people believed in clairvoyance, telepathy, and other psychic powers. However, with the advent of science and modern medicine, these beliefs were dismissed as superstition or pseudoscience.

This means that intuition enables us to perceive things beyond what we can physically see or hear. We may get a feeling about someone's true motives or pick up on subtle cues about a situation that we cannot explain rationally.

Intuition can also be described as a muscle- it gets stronger with regular use and practice. To tap into this intuitive ability requires living in curiosity about ourselves and the world around us. It means being open to experiences and actively seeking new perspectives rather than simply accepting or insisting upon what we think is true already.

We were all born knowing that we are perfect, whole, and complete. Then something happened... called life. As we grew up, many negative limiting beliefs were told to us about ourselves from well-meaning and not-so-well-meaning teachers, parents, and peers. We started to believe what they said was true: "I am not good enough or smart enough to make it." That thought got programmed into our consciousness and messed with our operating system.

As we grew up and became adults, we continued to operate unconsciously on these limiting and untrue belief systems we created as children. To free ourselves from those limitations and to live our lives guided by our sixth-sense intuition requires slowing down, silencing our [pre-recorded?] thoughts, and living in the present moment.

Essentially, it is about harnessing and focusing on the inner voice that guides us more fully through our lives. It is about listening to this voice that so often gets drowned out in the noise of daily life. Once we learn to tune into it regularly and let it guide our direction, we create a sense of clarity and inspiration that can lead us towards fulfilling lives both personally and professionally.

LOUISA JOVANOVICH

About Louisa Jovanovich: Louisa Jovanovich is a certified master hypnotist, intuitive coach, and transformational speaker who empowers individuals to break free from limiting beliefs and achieve their life vision. Born in Armenia and immigrating to the United States at age five, Louisa's early experiences of resilience significantly shaped her coaching approach. At seventeen, she discovered her gift for connection and healing while in a rehab center for an eating disorder, prompting her passion for personal development.

After nearly three decades as a successful hairstylist, Louisa's life took a transformative turn following the end of her fourteen-year marriage. She enrolled in the Clarity Catalyst program, an intensive course grounded in Stanford University's research on creativity and self-expression. This experience became the cornerstone of her coaching practice, leading her to become certified to teach the methodology.

Louisa further enhanced her skills at the Hypnosis Motivation Institute, creating a unique blend of intuitive coaching, hypnotherapy, and the Clarity Catalyst approach. As a co-author of thirteen bestselling books and host of the *Conscious Conversations Podcast*, Louisa reaches hundreds worldwide. Her philosophy blends mindset work, mindfulness practices, and intuitive mentorship, creating a nurturing space for dreams to take flight. "Your extraordinary life is waiting," she invites, encouraging others to ignite their potential.

Author's Website: *ConnectWithSource.com*

Book Series Website: *www.The13StepsToRiches.com*

Lynda Sunshine West

LISTEN, LYNDA, LISTEN

"My experience taught me that the next best thing to being truly great is to emulate the great, by feeling and action, as nearly as possible."
~ **Napoleon Hill**

Embracing the Sixth Sense in Life & Business

The human mind is capable of processing vast amounts of information, but there's a magic beyond logic—a "sixth sense" that whispers truths we can't always explain. We all have those gut feelings, those ideas that seem to leap out of nowhere but feel so right. For me, this sixth sense has become a trusted partner in both my life and business, and learning to listen to its messages has been absolutely transformational.

One defining moment came when I decided to break through a fear every single day for an entire year. Picture this: It's January 1, 2015. A woman, fifty-one years young, wakes up to a strong urge, "Fear is stopping me from living my life, so I'm going to break through one fear every day this year." What? Where did that come from?

It was from within my body that those words came out of my mouth. I hadn't been planning on breaking through fears. It just happened in that moment.

As you can imagine, I was staring my greatest fear in the face, the fear of breaking through fears. I had been content for the previous fifty-one years and had no desire to do anything different than what I had been doing (living a Groundhog Day life). The thought of breaking through one fear a day for an entire year terrified me and thrilled me at the same time. Deep down, a tiny voice urged, "Do it BECAUSE you're scared." I listened and took action.

I didn't know it then, but that was my sixth sense speaking to me.

That year was absolutely transformational. I met people I wouldn't have met, doors opened that I didn't know were closed, new paths were forged, and my entire life is different today (in a positive way) than it was before breaking through those fears.

Listening to our sixth sense can determine which road we walk down and who we meet. Who we meet can also affect our actions.

If you do a life review, do you recognize decisions you made that you now wish you hadn't because the result wasn't what you hoped it would be?

Next, as you think about those decisions, can you tie the steps you took into NOT listening to your sixth sense?

If your answer is "yes," here's where it gets good. You don't have to live that way anymore. You can choose to live a different life.

I started living my different life at age fifty-one and learned that you're never too old to embark on a new journey. You must make the decision to do so and then act on that decision. After all, nothing happens without action.

My decision to break through a fear every day for a year was just one of many moments when my sixth sense guided me into the unknown, inviting me to take action without necessarily having all the answers upfront.

In my career as a book publisher, this intuition has been my compass and has led me to meet incredible people and has introduced me to ideas that align perfectly with my mission to empower others by sharing their stories. It's taught me to look beyond the visible and to trust in both the mental and spiritual aspects of each opportunity. I'm passionate about helping others bring their stories to life, and through my journey with the sixth sense, I've seen how a single intuitive decision can lead to the most impactful results.

Forging a New Path

Napoleon Hill calls the sixth sense a "receiving set" through which thoughts, ideas, and solutions flash into the mind. I've come to see this as my creative engine, guiding me to thoughts I didn't even know I needed.

I remember the day I decided to pick up the bass guitar for the first time. I wasn't some fresh-faced teenager starting a hobby; I was forty-seven, and something about this challenge called to me on a soul level. People would ask, "Why the bass? Why now?" I didn't have a concrete answer; I just knew I felt called to do it.

In hindsight, it was my sixth sense nudging me toward something that would help me see myself in a new light. Playing bass wasn't just about music; it was about breaking through self-imposed limitations and trusting that initial spark of creative insight, no matter how unexpected it seemed. The sixth sense often leads us in ways we can't always explain at the moment, but looking back, I see it as one of the most consequential decisions I made for myself.

This experience with the bass guitar taught me that I didn't need a complete plan. I only needed to listen and take that first step, trusting that the rest would unfold. And boy, did it. Over the eight years our band, Useless Rhetoric, played, we raised over a quarter of a million dollars for charity. We became a charity band, and I fulfilled two passions: playing music and fundraising. I organized all of our charity events and found myself loving the organizational skills it took to put everything together and market the event so we could raise more money.

That one decision to start playing bass guitar led to so much more. I was stepping into the spotlight and getting myself ready for what was to come with my book publishing company (which I started ten years after learning to play bass guitar).

Over time, I started listening more closely to my sixth sense and taking actions without as much thought. They say, "Jump out of the plane and build it on your way down." While I think that's a crazy metaphor, I get it. If you're in alignment with the message and you do what you're being called to do, don't worry about how and just get out there and do it BECAUSE you're scared.

Recognizing & Responding to Hunches

The sixth sense doesn't come with a road map or a loudspeaker. It arrives in whispers, flashes, and what we often call "gut feelings" or "hunches." Those are the moments of knowing, where no logical explanation can account for the feeling that pulses through you. These flashes are gifts, nudging us toward opportunities or away from dangers, and learning to recognize them has been one of the greatest tools in my life.

From a young age, I had an inkling of this sixth sense, though it was often colored by fear. When I ran away at the age of five, staying away for a week, I came home with a very different perspective. Fear crept in, and I quickly grew accustomed to a people-pleasing life. In the years that followed, I almost forgot the voice of intuition, muffling it under layers of caution and (because of my tremendous fear of judgment) a desire to "fit in." But that sense of knowing was always there, waiting for me to tap into it fully.

During my year of breaking through a fear every day, I noticed something remarkable: as I leaned into the discomfort, my sixth sense became sharper, clearer. It wasn't buried under anxiety or doubt anymore. Instead, it was there to remind me, "You've got this," giving me strength in moments I couldn't have anticipated.

Today, I encourage others—especially the authors I work with—to listen to their own intuitive flashes. So often, our doubts and fears try to silence that voice, convincing us to "play it safe" or "stick to what we know." I've learned that the more we act on the nudges coming to us from within, the clearer and more frequent they become. And that's what I call "living."

In those moments when the logical mind hesitates, the sixth sense says, "Go for it." These hunches are the bridge between our goals and our greatest potential. Does this mean we shouldn't listen to the logical mind? No, not at all. This is more about listening and making a decision from a place of awareness. I believe the sixth sense is a guiding light that leads us toward the life we're truly meant to live.

Strengthening the Sixth Sense Daily

The sixth sense is a mysterious yet powerful guide. Through the sixth sense, I've learned that we don't always need to know exactly where we're going; we only need to take the next step, trusting that our inner guidance will light the way.

I invite you to listen to your sixth sense daily, honor it, and let it become a trusted partner on your journey. Embrace the unknown, lean into your passions, and allow your inner wisdom to lead you toward the life you are truly meant to live. Remember, every great accomplishment begins with a single step of faith.

LYNDA SUNSHINE WEST

About Lynda Sunshine West: As the Founder and CEO of Action Takers Publishing, Lynda Sunshine West's mission is to empower five million women and men to share their stories with the world to make a greater impact on the planet. She is affectionately known as The Queen of Collaboration. Lynda Sunshine is a Book Publisher, Speaker, Multiple Times #1 International Bestselling Author, Executive Film Producer, and Red Carpet Interviewer.

At the age of five, she ran away and was gone an entire week. She came home riddled with fears that stopped her from living and, in turn, became a people-pleaser. At age fifty-one, she decided to break through one fear every day for a year. In doing so, she gained an exorbitant amount of confidence and now uses what she learned to fulfill her mission. She believes in cooperation and collaboration and loves connecting with like-minded people.

Author's Website: *www.ActionTakersPublishing.com*

Book Series Website: *www.The13StepstoRiches.com*

Maris Segal & Ken Ashby

THE TRUST FEAR DICHOTOMY: UNLOCKING THE POWER OF INTUITION

We have learned from Napoleon Hill that the sixth sense is "that portion of the subconscious mind which has been referred to as Creative Imagination." Our sixth sense can be developed through the use of imagination and intuition. By focusing on our goals and visualizing ourselves as having already achieved them, we can tap into this powerful inner resource and use it to guide and manifest our desires.

Hill doubles down by calling our "sixth sense" the "power tool" for personal growth and success. Accessing this power tool invites us to trust our imagination, trust our inner voice, trust our gut, and trust our intuition. In doing so, we can begin to become aware of our "relationship with trust."

Maris: During my college years, on a journalism scholarship, I felt certain that my true life's path was to be a reporter. Thinking that that the best way to fulfill my dream was to give voice to issues, causes, and brands that were "doing good" and empowering humanity. However, I experienced a moment when my inner voice, my "sixth sense," compelled me to make a choice. It was a flash of clarity that changed the trajectory of my life!

I took a break from my journalism studies to accept a position on a small team designing and managing the Olympic Torch Relay preceding the

1984 Olympic Games in Los Angeles. At twenty-two years old, I was the youngest selected from hundreds who interviewed nationally. I was honored and also felt immense pressure to live up to "what the heck the leadership saw in me."

Our mission was to connect the Olympics to communities far and wide in a torch relay that would feature local runners and raise funds for local charities. To this day, this has been one of the most challenging and best jobs I've ever had! I was responsible for the twelve-hundred-mile route from Seattle to Los Angeles.

In that time, there were no cell phones, email was just a toddler, and document sharing came with the beeps and burring noises of a dial-up fax modem. Creating the driving route and sponsored portions called for specific measurements and meant using rudimentary calculators and paper maps that must have been folded by an origami master!

Nearing the completion of the eighty-two-day Torch Relay, now just days before the torch was to arrive at the LA Colosseum for opening ceremonies, Olympic fever was swelling! We had thousands of people three-five rows deep lining the route to see and experience the actual Olympic flame passing by. Press coverage had increased over the miles, days, and months, as this was the first and only opportunity for many people to participate in this historic Olympic event.

We were just outside of Los Angeles and, just as we had done in other large cities, "flatbed trucks" for the press and camera crews were offered so they could cover the runner's caravan in "real-time." As the relay continued, timed down to the minute, our challenge became slowing the caravan down long enough for the press to get through the crowds and safely board the already packed media flatbed. As new reporters arrived there was constant pushing and scrambling for position. It all just got a bit too crazy and, more importantly, unsafe.

While watching the pushing and shoving and hearing shouting disgruntled public, from kids to seniors, and the press, I experienced a small voice inside me, "Is this really the way you want to unite and empower humanity?" When my Olympic job ended, so did my interest in being a reporter. It was in that "flatbed moment" that I realized, in a flash of clarity, that I did not want to spend my career climbing over people and fighting for position just to get the story.

I would find another way to fulfill my professional desires and impact lives for the greater good. It was the use and trust of that "power tool," my sixth sense that completely altered the trajectory of my life. I listened to my intuition and faced my fears of changing direction, disappointing my parents, criticism from teachers, and creating a source of income.

We are in a relationship with ourselves 24/7, and if we don't trust ourselves, how will others trust us? Why do we find it so difficult to trust that innermost feeling, our voice? Hill said that we get stopped by "fear," and he provided six primary fears: Poverty, Criticism, Ill Health, Loss of Love, Old Age, and Death. Stealing the title of a recent movie, these basic human "fears" grab hold and influence us with *"everything, everywhere, all at once!"*

Our "relationship" with trust can be improved to dislodge old stories and paralyzing fears that hold us back. In our work as Relational Leadership and Business coaches, trainers, and speakers, we have identified four Universal Relationship Rhythms: Respect, Responsibility, Reframing, and Resilience. When these rhythms are working in-sync throughout our day, in a circular motion of energy, our lives are thriving and prospering.

To grow a healthy relationship with trust and start to conquer our fears, we can use the universal rhythm of "Reframing." To reframe limiting beliefs and old stories created from traumas and dramas in our lives, we lead with gratitude; we accept the experiences of our past without letting them limit us, we meet people where they are, and we honor feedback. When we reframe, a new perspective emerges, and a shift happens!

Reframing Fears & Choosing to Trust Your Inner Voice

What is fear really, have you ever heard this one? Fear = False Evidence Appearing Real. We can choose instead to FACE what we're feeling— Freely Acknowledge Current Emotions and trust our "sixth sense," that voice inside that calls us to step forward.

The **fear of poverty** and living in a place of not having "enough" can be paralyzing and often hold us back from acting and pursuing our dreams.

Reframing: We can choose to *reframe* the stories we've told ourselves about the possibility of financial ruin and replace that fear with curiosity and listening to our imagination, seeing and feeling our financial success with specificity as if it has already happened.

The **fear of criticism** often stems from a deep-seated need for approval and validation from others and a fear of rejection or disapproval.

Reframing: We can choose to welcome criticism as valued feedback and listen to the voice inside that says, "I can learn something from this moment," and turn what didn't work into your next winning accomplishment.

The **fear of ill health** is often rooted in a desire to control the uncertainty in our lives, which can be challenged by the unpredictable nature of our bodies and the potential for illness or injury.

Reframing: Overcoming this fear requires a shift in mindset towards self-acceptance and choosing to hear what our bodies are telling us. We can counteract this anxiety by hearing our voice of "gratitude and thankfulness" for our amazing body and all its parts.

The **fear of loss of love** or broken relationships is a powerful force that can hold us back from pursuing our desires and living our best lives. This fear is rooted in our basic human need for connection and acceptance, which is often tied to our sense of self-worth and identity.

Reframing: Choosing to hear the voice inside that says, "Something is not in-sync in this relationship," builds trust in yourself. Instead of being a victim, we can choose to recognize our personal "responsibility" in the outcome and stand victorious.

The **fear of old age** is a common and understandable concern for many people. This fear can limit our willingness to take risks or try new things.

Reframing: Rather than seeing ourselves as aging out because of a perceived limitation of *old age*, we can choose to live in "respect" of the wisdom that a full life produces. Trusting our inner voice that says, "I am not done," offers new opportunities to share our wisdom and keep learning from life.

The **fear of death** is fundamental and universal, and it influences the way we live our lives and pursue our dreams. This is because death represents the ultimate unknown and the ultimate loss. No one lives forever—physically, that is!

Reframing: What we choose to bring to life during our present existence will most certainly be the legacy we leave for future generations. Listen to the voice inside that says, "Today, I get to do something new and life-giving." Reframing the fear of death actually allows us to live, contribute, and receive more fully.

It is astounding to imagine what we can accomplish when we are not held in the vise-grip of fear and listen instead to our intuition. Working through our fears is not a one-and-done situation. It is constant and as consistent as change. We cannot control change or the challenging situations we may face. We can control our mindset and our actions.

"Trust your instincts, and they will never fail you."

Reflections:

1. Over the past few years, note when you trusted your "sixth sense" and when you didn't.

2. Of the six primary fears, which are holding you in a tight grip?

3. Letting go of the fear of dying, what steps can you take today to spend your time truly living?

MARIS SEGAL & KEN ASHBY

About Ken Ashby & Maris Segal: From Mindset to Marketing, Ken Ashby and Maris Segal, a husband and wife dynamic duo, have spent the last thirty-plus years bringing an innovative, collaborative voice to issues, causes, and brands. As entrepreneurs, activists, business strategists, executive producers, coaches, authors, speakers, and trainers, Ken and Maris work with the public and private sectors from boardrooms and classrooms to the world stage. They are known for creating high-touch experiences that unite diverse populations across a broad spectrum of business, policy, and social issues.

Their leadership expertise in Business Relationship Marketing, Organizational Change & Cultural Inclusion, Personal Growth, Project Management, Public Affairs, and Philanthropy Strategies has been called upon by companies and their agencies. Their experience includes: consumer and financial brands, Olympic organizers, Super Bowls, America's 400th Anniversary, Harvard Kennedy School, Archdiocese of LA and NY Papal visit planners, the White House and celebrities across the arts, entertainment, sports, and culinary genres. With Ken's expertise as an award-winning singer-songwriter, they launched ONE SONG, a songwriting workshop series designed to unleash creativity in individuals and teams.

Their **DRIVE** method: **D**esire, **R**elationships, **I**ntention, **V**ision and **E**mpowerment sits at the core of their companies Prosody Creative Services, ONE SONG, and Segal Leadership Global to set a path for every client to Build High Performing Businesses and Elevate Personal and Professional Leadership for Maximum Impact and a 360-degree Thriving Life!

Author's Website: *www.SegalLeadershipGlobal.com*
Book Series Website: *www.The13StepsToRiches.com*

Mel Mason

TUNING INTO THE UNIVERSE'S FREQUENCY

The Universe is constantly broadcasting subtle signals that are meant to guide us along the right path. The problem for most of us is that we have too much internal interference cluttering our airwaves. But once we deal with our broadcast interference, we find and reconnect with the Universe's frequency.

Once we declutter our broadcast of all interferences, dissolving any limited beliefs we have, we're left with a crystal clear line of communication. We're better positioned to emit high-frequency broadcasts to others. As we collect messages from the ether, we're free to either accept or dismiss the broadcasts we receive from the world around us. And the clearer our broadcast is, the more likely we are to pick up the subtle signals the Universe sends. This is our sixth sense.

According to Napoleon Hill, the sixth sense is the portion of the subconscious mind referred to as the Creative Imagination. Our sixth sense allows us to subconsciously receive broadcasts from the ether and, in a flash, turn them into ideas, plans, and thoughts.

Most of us have had some interaction with our sixth sense before, even if we didn't realize it in the moment. The "flashes" are often called hunches, inspirations, or even a gut feeling. They're the split-second waves of thoughts and emotions we experience in times of crisis. They wash over us to force a reality check.

There are a million thoughts racing through our minds at any given second. Allowing the now means clearing those thoughts away and focusing on the moment we're in. We stop thinking about what's coming up at work, what errands we have to run later, and what's on the calendar for the week. Those thoughts are cluttering our space to allow the now.

Allowing the now clears the line of communication our sixth sense uses to collect messages from the Universe. Think of allowing the now as turning the knob on your internal radio to clear the static away. Allowing the now helps us tune in to what the Universe is trying to tell us.

It's tempting to tune out our sixth sense when it sends messages at inconvenient times. Low-frequency thoughts and ideas clutter our space, making us more likely to push off messages from the Universe. The flashes aren't always comfortable or convenient. If our intuition tells us to slow down and change course, we won't listen if doing so means we end up late to a meeting. We won't reschedule an appointment for a gut feeling. Our instinct is to shake the feeling off, avoid the now, and press on…even if it means putting ourselves in danger.

I still remember the first time I accessed my sixth sense. When I was little, I lived near a cemetery. It was a massive piece of property with tombstones dating back hundreds of years. I used to play in it all the time, running through the rows of crumbling rocks and admiring the flowers left for loved ones. It sounds macabre, but it was innocent fun for a little girl.

One day, though, as I went to play, I got this feeling like I wasn't supposed to be there. The feeling washed over me. My limbs felt rigid. My pulse fluttered faster than usual. I didn't understand what the feeling meant, so I pressed on and went to play like always.

As I strolled through the rows of tombstones, I heard a low rumble coming from the main gate. I looked up and saw a figure on top of a motorcycle tearing down the road toward me. I didn't think much of it at first—other people visit the cemetery, too—until the bike came off the pavement and sped over the grass in my direction. It cut through the rows between us, and I knew it was coming for me.

My limbs unlocked, and I tore off in the opposite direction. I could hear the motorcycle gaining on me but didn't dare look back. I reached the top of a big hill and threw myself down the other side, desperate to get away. I barreled down the hill as thorn bushes raked at my arms and rocks crunched against my toes. I couldn't feel any of it. I had to get away.

I kept running until I was safely out of the cemetery and took shelter in a thicket of trees. I stayed there for hours—long after I stopped hearing the motorcycle's engine. I walked back home just as the sun started to set, covered in cuts and bruises.

I have no idea what would have happened to me if the figure on the motorcycle had caught up to me. I don't know their intentions, and I likely never will. All I know is that when the Universe tried to warn me about danger, I ignored it until it was almost too late.

Now that I'm older, I better understand my sixth sense, but that doesn't mean I'm always good at listening. Take my most recent near-death experience, for example. On my drive home from celebrating completing my thesis with friends, there was a moment where my intuition, my sixth sense, warned me to turn back. There was another, safer path I could've taken home, one without the risk of freezing roads. But that route was a longer drive, so I chose not to change course. I compromised with the Universe and drove under the speed limit.

My sixth sense told me not to follow through with my plan, but instead of listening, I thought I was smarter than the Universe. I thought I was being careful. I saw the temperature drop on my truck's gauge. I knew I was moving through a dangerous area. I thought driving slowly would save me, but that patch of ice still sent me spinning.

I recently returned to the spot where my truck spun off the road. It was alongside the edge of a cliff, and in broad daylight, I could see there were hardly any spots where a car could careen down the mountainside. Giant boulders, trees, and debris would catch anything that fell off the road. However, the one spot where I *started* sliding was one of the only places with an open space to fall straight down the cliff.

My saving grace was the compromise I made with the Universe. By slowing down, my spinout was slow enough to allow my truck to bounce off the small curb between the road and the cliffside. Hitting that curb spun my truck around 180 degrees and parallel parked me between the only two Manzanita trees on the other side.

Our sixth sense is always there collecting broadcasts from the Universe. It's not a magical tool that is only accessed through some spell or ritual. The only skill we need to access our sixth sense is active listening. Hear what the Universe has to say, then do what it says to do. At the very least, you'll save some money on car insurance deductibles!

With as many near-death experiences as I've had, you'd think I'd be paranoid the Universe is out to get me. The truth is, I believe the opposite. I believe the Universe has a plan for me, and until that plan is finished, nothing's going to take me out—not a car accident, not an emotional breakdown, and not even a spooky, motorcycle-bound monster barreling through a cemetery.

Everything comes down to desire. I have a desire to live, so I live. I have a desire to complete my mission on this planet, so I deliver my message every day. My desire to enact positive change vibrates on the same frequency as the Universe. I am a small part of a greater plan. As long as I have the desire to follow the plan the best I can, nothing's going to stop me.

I've said it before and I'll say it again: no one makes it out of life unscathed. It takes great effort and mindfulness to avoid being unhappy. It's easy to vibrate at a low frequency, let the clutter fill our space, and ignore the bigger picture of the world around us. We're all excellent at burying our pain beneath clutter and hiding it from plain sight. We are masters at distracting ourselves from our own clutter—some of us use alcohol, some of us use our work, and others even use other people's clutter as an excuse to avoid their own.

As the Clutter Expert, I've mastered the ability to remove anything that gets in the way of my relationship with the Universe. Messages flow in and out of our conscious and subconscious all the time. If we ignore them, they pile up around us, and the clutter gets out of control. Clutter is inevitable, but removing it is how we stay in touch with the Universe. When clutter appears, we take a closer look at where it came from and what it means to us. Only then can we remove it, either by throwing it away or putting it in its rightful place.

When you finally listen to your sixth sense and start in on your own clutter, remember to be kind to yourself. Be mindful. Turn off the autosuggestions telling you this task is too big, too hard, or too painful. Lean on your mastermind for support. Make decisions to keep or toss your clutter, then make more.

The more space you clear, the more room your imagination has to flourish, and the clearer the Universe's message for you comes through. Before you know it, you'll see a path open up in front of you—one full of joy, abundance, and a Universe filled with love.

MEL MASON

About Mel Mason: International Bestselling Author Mel Mason is The Clutter Expert, and as a sexual abuse survivor, she grew up depressed, suicidal, and surrounded by clutter. What she realized after coming back from the brink of despair and getting through her own chaos was that the outside is just a mirror of the inside, and if you only address the outside without changing the inside, the clutter keeps coming back.

That set her on a mission to empower people around the world to get free from clutter inside and out, so they can experience happiness and abundance in every area of their lives.

She is the author of *Freedom from Clutter: The Guaranteed, Foolproof, Step-by-Step Process to Remove the Stuff That's Weighing You Down.*

Author's Website: *www.FreeGiftFromMel.com*

Book Series Website: *www.The13StepsToRiches.com*

Michael D. Butler

IF I ONLY HAD AN INTUITIVE BRAIN

"If I Only Had a Brain."
~ **Scarecrow**

The Young Brain: Key to the Future

Did you receive adequate brain stimulation as a child? Did someone read to you? Did you have a tutor? Did you have learning disabilities? Were you in advanced placement classes? Were you breastfed?

Give Your Babies the Neuro Edge

When you consider Adam's first job in the Bible, it was beyond the College/Doctoral level; it was far beyond what you'd expect a single individual or team of individuals armed with the latest technology to complete. That job was naming all the animals. That's right, name every species, every variation of every animal, every bird, every fish, every type of marine life and sea creature, every type of mammal and four-footed insect, reptile, snake, turtle, etc.

The number of animal species is vast and estimated to be millions. It shows you the tremendous capacity he had to create, remember, and expand his brain function. This story truly shows us what is possible. I hypothesize that brain development should be a life-long pursuit.

Did you know 85% of brain development happens in the first five years of life?

Yes, that's correct. The early years of a child's life are crucial for brain development. Research indicates that a significant portion of neural development occurs during the first few years, shaping the foundation for cognitive, emotional, and social abilities. The experiences and interactions during this period play a vital role in establishing neural connections and pathways.

The best thing parents and caregivers can give young children is attention: Attention by listening, asking questions, and observing. By letting a child talk, think, ask questions, and explore a child is gathering the information necessary to help them navigate the world. Like a computational computer, the hard drive of their brain is working at an ever increasingly rapid rate of speed to gather information, analyze information, and make sense of that information.

Limit screen time for young children. Studies are ongoing and vary and they don't always agree. While it is easy for a busy parent to use digital content like iPads, smartphones, and computers to help babysit our children, it's important to know what children are watching, playing, and doing online. Age appropriate is the big thing here, and parental monitoring is paramount for the child's safety and, of course, ultimate brain development, which will come from real conversations with other real humans.

While it's true that breast milk is widely recognized for its nutritional benefits for infants, and it contains essential nutrients that support overall development, including brain development, it's important to note that scientific research often emphasizes the multifaceted nature of factors influencing brain development.

The social side of brain development happens when an infant bonds with the mother during breastfeeding time through eye contact, facial recognition, and non-verbal communication. There are volumes of studies that show children who are breastfed have many neurological advantages.

Americans are Not Reading & How to Fix It

A full 85% of college graduates never buy or read another book after college graduation in the USA. This may stem from 8 or more semesters of buying overpriced textbooks in the college bookstore. Seventy-six percent of books in English are bought and read outside of the USA, and 65-70% of global book consumption is fiction, with 30-35% being non-fiction books, according to Bowker.

I'm not sure how we fix it. You can lead a horse to water, but you can't make him drink but you can put salt in his oats. It's not until a person wants to change their learn and change their life that they'll be motivated to do it.

Are You Only Using 10% of Your Brain?

The idea that we only use 10% of our brains is a common misconception. Neuroscientific research has consistently shown that the entire brain is active, and each part has a specific function. While it's true that not all regions of the brain are active simultaneously, there is no evidence to support the claim that we only use a small percentage of our brains.

No doubt our brain is capable of far more than most humans tax it for. Imagine when it comes to learning new languages, playing musical instruments, and solving complex math, and philosophical problems. the human brain has historically exhibited the propensity for genius and beyond.

Seeing what an individual brain can accomplish alone makes us only wonder the potential that is possible when many human brains think and act in tandem. Could the collective brain become infinite in that regard?

However, if you're interested in enhancing cognitive abilities and optimizing brain function, here are some evidence-based strategies:

Lifelong Learning

Engage in continuous learning and intellectual stimulation. Acquiring new skills, taking up new hobbies, and pursuing educational activities can help create new neural connections and maintain cognitive flexibility.

Physical Exercise

Regular exercise has been linked to improved cognitive function, including memory, attention, and executive function. Exercise increases blood flow to the brain and promotes the release of neurotransmitters that support cognitive health.

Adequate Sleep

Quality sleep is essential for cognitive function and memory consolidation. Ensure you get enough restorative sleep each night to support overall brain health.

Healthy Diet

Eat a balanced and nutritious diet that includes omega-3 fatty acids, antioxidants, and other essential nutrients. These nutrients support brain health and can contribute to optimal cognitive function.

Mindfulness & Meditation

Practices such as mindfulness meditation have been associated with changes in brain structure and function. Regular meditation can improve attention, reduce stress, and enhance overall well-being.

Social Connections

Maintain strong social connections and engage in meaningful relationships. Social interaction is beneficial for cognitive health and emotional well-being.

Challenging Mental Activities

Engage in activities that challenge your cognitive abilities. This could include puzzles, brain games, or complex problem-solving tasks.

Reduce Stress

Chronic stress can have negative effects on the brain. Adopt stress-management techniques such as deep breathing, yoga, or other relaxation methods to promote brain health.

Stay Hydrated

Proper hydration is crucial for optimal brain function. Dehydration can impair cognitive abilities, so ensure you are drinking enough water throughout the day.

Brain-Boosting Supplements

Some supplements, such as omega-3 fatty acids, vitamin B complex, and antioxidants, may support brain health. Consult with a healthcare professional before adding supplements to your routine.

It's important to note that individual responses to these strategies may vary, and there is no one-size-fits-all approach. Additionally, maintaining overall health and well-being is key to supporting cognitive function. If you have specific concerns or are considering major lifestyle changes, it's advisable to consult with a healthcare professional or a qualified expert in the field.

Preventing Alzheimer's & Dementia

Alzheimer's disease and dementia are significant global health challenges, affecting millions of people. According to the World Health Organization (WHO), around fifty million people worldwide were estimated to be living with dementia in 2020, and this number is expected to nearly triple by 2050.

Preventing Alzheimer's and dementia involves a combination of lifestyle choices, early detection, and management of risk factors. Here are some key strategies:

Healthy Lifestyle

Adopting a healthy lifestyle is crucial. This includes regular physical exercise, a balanced diet rich in fruits and vegetables, and maintaining a healthy weight. Aerobic exercise has been associated with a lower risk of cognitive decline.

Cognitive Stimulation

Engage in mentally stimulating activities, such as reading, solving puzzles, learning new skills, or playing musical instruments. Keeping the brain active may contribute to cognitive resilience.

Heart-Healthy Diet

A diet that is good for the heart is also considered beneficial for the brain. This includes a diet low in saturated fats, trans fats, and cholesterol. The Mediterranean and DASH diets, which emphasize fruits, vegetables, whole grains, and lean proteins, are often recommended.

Social Engagement

Maintain social connections and engage in activities that involve interaction with others. Social engagement has been linked to a lower risk of cognitive decline.

Quality Sleep

Prioritize good sleep hygiene. Poor sleep patterns, including sleep apnea, have been associated with a higher risk of cognitive decline.

Management of Chronic Conditions

Control and manage chronic conditions such as diabetes, hypertension, and high cholesterol. These conditions can impact vascular health, which in turn can affect brain health.

Moderate Alcohol Consumption

If alcohol is consumed, do so in moderation. Excessive alcohol intake can increase the risk of cognitive decline.

Avoid Smoking

Smoking is associated with an increased risk of cognitive decline. Quitting smoking can have multiple health benefits, including reducing the risk of dementia.

Mental Health

Manage stress and prioritize mental health. Chronic stress can contribute to cognitive decline, so adopting stress-reduction techniques is important.

Regular Health Check-ups

Regular health check-ups can help in the early detection and management of any health conditions that could contribute to cognitive decline.

It's important to note that while these strategies may reduce the risk of Alzheimer's and dementia, they don't guarantee prevention.

For the most current and personalized information, it's recommended to consult healthcare professionals and stay informed about ongoing research and developments in the field of neurology and cognitive health.

But the truth is you can improve and preserve your mental function and cognitive ability. Keep your mind young. Talk to young people, travel, read different kinds of books, take different routes to work, and brush your teeth for 30 days with the "other" hand. Say your ABCs backward, count to 1 from 100 backward, and work on crossword puzzles and other exciting games that stimulate the brain. Learn a foreign language, learn some new dance moves, or a new and different musical instrument. This will all go a long way to help rewire the synapsis of your brain and to improve neuroplasticity.

MICHAEL D. BUTLER

About Michael D. Butler: Called the Simon Cowell of Book Publishing, celebrity kingmaker Michael D. Butler is most proud of his four sons and two grandsons. His authors have spoken in fifty countries.

As a global book publisher and speaker, Butler is a recognized authority in the book publishing space, with 794 titles published by authors in sixty-four nations. Helping authors and speakers evolve and create platforms of influence in an ever-changing marketplace.

Founder of 1040Impact.org has rescued 394 girls from human trafficking ages 6-17, caring for them in a safe, loving environment with a full-time staff of twenty-five in Pakistan.

Author's Website: *www.MichaelDButler.com*

Book Series Website: *www.The13StepsToRiches.com*

Michelle Cameron Coulter & Al Coulter

CULTIVATING THE SIXTH SENSE: TRUSTING THE UNSEEN

The Power of Connection

How many of us believe in a larger connection between people? In nature, we see it frequently—birds and fish moving as one, sensing each other's rhythms without words. It's a form of communication that goes beyond language, almost like a shared consciousness—a sixth sense.

This type of connection, which my wife Michelle and I have experienced on many levels, goes beyond mere instinct. We recently watched Tyler Henry, a medium who brings forward messages that feel deeply personal to those he connects with. Witnessing his work was a powerful reminder that there is a connection between us all, something both subtle and profound, ready to reveal itself to those who remain open.

One experience that has stayed with us involves our son, who, like many children, seemed to have an open and clear connection to this sixth sense. During my father's final weeks, our kids spent significant time with him, sharing precious moments. On the night my father passed away, our son —who was just five or six at the time—sat straight up in bed and called out his grandpa's name.

Later, we realized this happened at the exact moment my father took his last breath. Somehow, he simply knew. Children often embody a pure version of this intuition; they haven't yet learned to question or rationalize it away. As adults, with so many distractions and pressures, we sometimes lose touch with this innate knowing, but moments like these remind us it's always there, waiting to be heard.

We might not all have the kind of intuition Tyler Henry shows, but we do have access to a unique version of it through intuition, our "gut feelings," and even our empathy. In our journey, learning to connect in this deeper way has been transformative. We've come to see that this "sixth sense" is not just something otherworldly or mysterious—it's a skill we can develop and refine through practice.

Listening to Your Gut: The Gift of Intuition

We've all heard the advice to "trust your gut." This phrase captures our sixth sense in its purest form, and the more we listen, the sharper it becomes. I remember a lesson in this during one of my early business ventures. I had partnered with someone whose integrity I began to question. I couldn't quite pinpoint why, but my stomach would churn whenever I thought about certain things he did. And sure enough, while Michelle and I were away, I lost my share of the company as my partner had secretly transferred everything out.

At first, it was a hard blow to take. I struggled to understand it until one of my mentors, Jim Rohn, taught me something life-changing. "Negative things will happen," he said, "and you have two choices: let it beat you down or treat it as a lesson."

Over time, I realized it was a profound lesson in listening to my intuition. It wasn't just a loss; it was a push toward something greater. From that moment forward, I leaned into my intuition and built my next company twice the size of the first.

But the journey didn't end there. I started noticing that familiar feeling, a stirring in my gut around some of my new partners. I chose to ignore it, thinking I had already learned my lesson. This time, though, the lesson returned with even more clarity—listen to the signals your gut is sending.

Honing Your Sixth Sense Through Connection

Our sixth sense also sharpens when we invest in understanding others. In a world that often focuses on quick texts and surface-level conversations, taking the time to go deeper is rare yet invaluable. I think of this as listening "between the lines"—reading body language, sensing energy, or even feeling someone's intentions without words.

Michelle and I have noticed that asking people intentional questions like, "What is truly important to you right now? Have you taken time to tell the people you love how proud you are of them?" brings forward a sense of connection that often unlocks the sixth sense. The moment you go beyond small talk, you start picking up on things that weren't explicitly said. You learn to read the energy, the pauses, and even the silence.

This is what trusting your sixth sense can do: it makes you aware of others on a level that transcends words. It encourages a different kind of communication that lets you "see" beyond what is spoken.

Cultivating Your Sixth Sense Daily

Our sixth sense is like a muscle that grows stronger with use. Whether you're working to enhance intuition, empathy, or gut instinct, there are daily practices that can help you cultivate this inner skill. Here are some ways to incorporate it into your life:

1. Practice Presence

In our fast-paced world, presence is becoming a lost art. Spend time with yourself and others without distractions. Even just a few minutes a day where you're entirely present—whether during meditation, deep breathing, or spending quiet time outdoors—can make a significant impact. When we are fully present, we tune into a deeper awareness, allowing our sixth sense to flourish.

For instance, try turning off your phone during dinner or stepping outside without any devices. These small acts bring our awareness into the present and, over time, hone our intuition.

2. Listen Without Words

Next time you're in conversation, focus on the other person's energy rather than just their words. Notice their tone, expressions, and body language. Ask open-ended questions and let the conversation flow. When you're attuned in this way, you start to notice when people feel disconnected, stressed, or especially passionate about something. You might feel a sense of empathy or a gentle nudge to ask a deeper question, which often reveals the things that matter most.

3. Trust Small Impressions

It's common to brush off subtle impressions, thinking they're unimportant or imaginary. But when you feel a nudge or get a sense about something, take it seriously. Trusting these small impressions, whether it's a feeling of excitement or a sense of discomfort, can be the key to uncovering valuable insights.

As you become more attuned, you'll recognize these small impressions as an essential part of your sixth sense. Start by observing these impressions during routine activities—like choosing a route to work or deciding when to call someone back—and see where they lead you.

4. Reflect & Learn from Past Experiences

Set aside time to reflect on decisions where you followed (or ignored) your intuition. Write down any recurring feelings or thoughts and think about the outcomes. Reflection helps us recognize patterns and builds confidence in our gut instinct. Over time, this reflection will strengthen your trust in this sense and make it easier to listen in the future. For example, think back on choices you made that felt "off" or moments when you felt in perfect alignment; both help you understand your intuitive strengths.

5. Express Your Inner Voice

One of the biggest challenges people face in developing their sixth sense is learning to express what they feel. If something doesn't sit right with you, give yourself permission to acknowledge it—even if you don't fully understand why. Speaking up about your intuition with close friends or loved ones can help you refine and trust it.

Living with a Sixth Sense Mindset

When we embrace the sixth sense as a mindset, it becomes a way of life rather than just a skill. This mindset shapes how we interact with others, make decisions, and view ourselves in the world. Having a sixth sense means trusting that there is a flow guiding us, even when things don't go as planned. Sometimes, a closed door is simply a redirection toward a better path.

Developing this mindset doesn't mean you'll never make mistakes. In fact, the sixth sense often grows stronger through trial and error. Each setback, each time we fail to listen to our intuition, we learn and evolve. These lessons remind us that even when our path seems unclear, our inner voice is there to guide us, one nudge at a time.

Conclusion: Honoring Your Sixth Sense

Our sixth sense is an incredible guide, a part of ourselves that can be a compass through life. Each lesson, each moment of listening, is an invitation to lean into that mysterious but undeniable connection we all share. Ultimately, it's about recognizing the depth of our connections—to ourselves and others—and choosing to trust them.

When we listen deeply, whether to our gut, our hearts, or those we care about, we honor something beyond words. In doing so, we become a greater version of ourselves, fully aligned and attuned to the unseen but powerful forces that help shape our lives.

xo
~ Michelle and Al

MICHELLE CAMERON COULTER & AL COULTER

About Michelle Cameron Coulter: Michelle is an Olympic gold medalist, entrepreneur, mother of four, community leader raising millions of dollars for charities, global inspirational leader, and founder and CEO of Inspiring Possibilities.

About Al Coulter: Al is a two-time Olympian in volleyball, captain of Team Canada, world record holder in matches representing one's country in any sport, with over 735 matches, entrepreneur, father of four, and personal best coach, specializing in relationships, team, and resilience.

Michelle and Al are the embodiment of today's leaders. Strong and empowering, they embraced life's challenges with strength and courage. They bring insight, compassion, depth, and inspiration to the table with multiple world championships, three Olympics, an Olympic gold medal, marriage, and four children.

They are sought-after inspirational leaders. Through their speaking, workshops, and retreats, their gift and passion is to "inspire possibilities" and encourage people to embrace their greatness in a real, authentic, healthy, and vibrant way—creating thriving community, connection, and one's own gold medal results.

Author's Website: *www.MichelleCameronCoulter.com*

Book Series Website: *www.The13StepsToRiches.com*

Dr. Michelle Mras

A DUCK IS A DUCK... OR IS IT?

The subconscious mind is the most powerful tool in your arsenal to achieve success. We have read throughout the series of *The 13 Steps to Riches*, based on the *Think and Grow Rich* by Napoleon Hill, that behind each of the twelve prior steps, success requires the ability to master one's mind. Our thoughts, beliefs, and emotions are fueled by the subconscious mind.

It is imperative that we make a conscious effort to listen and obtain guidance from our subconscious. Without this step, the manifesting of the intangible into the tangible is lost. The manifestation is accomplished through the use of imagination, visualization, auto-suggestion, and affirmations. We need our conscious mind to align with our subconscious mind to transform our dreams into reality. Without the subconscious, our goals are merely dreams.

Each of us has a sixth sense. At what level of awareness we work, this sixth sense varies. It helps us make decisions very quickly based on our past experiences. As a professional speaker, thought leader, author, and entertainer, I run in circles of individuals who persistently seek self-improvement. We often speak about, "What does your gut say?" or "What is your first instinct reaction?" It never occurred to me that someone would not think in terms of seeking self-improvement.

This is why I was caught off guard when a woman approached me to say she had no idea what I was speaking about. I mentioned "gut instinct" and "intuition" during my talk on stage. She was quite a logical woman. She informed me that she doesn't make decisions based on feelings;

rather, she uses facts. This "woo hoo" adaption of making decisions off indigestion troubled her. We talked for quite a while and she explained her process of making decisions. She mentioned how she takes all the data she can collect into account to make a decision. I said, "That is an educated guess. This is your intuition!" Her face lit up, knowing that she did have her version of "gut feelings."

We discussed further as I compared her logic to how "gut feelings" are a subconscious assessment of everything she had ever learned, heard, witnessed, experienced, read, etc. In essence, no one is truly using an emotional trigger; we are accessing our subconscious mind at such a high rate that we don't recognize the process as a checklist of what we have come to know but rather a quick, united response to all that our subconscious has compiled. That explanation helped both of us that day.

As I further pondered the power of the unconscious mind, I realized that although it allows us to make decisions quickly, they are not always the right ones. Sometimes, our past, especially if it is traumatic, can have an oversized effect on us. I have a perfect example of my "gut feeling" negatively affecting my logical thoughts.

About two months into the COVID-19 lockdown, I used the worldwide lockdown to evaluate my life and the trajectory of my career as a professional speaker in a world without live conferences. Like many of us, I was connecting with people on social media, but I needed human contact. I sought communities to feed my soul and mind.

As I was browsing through a social media site, I saw a face pop-up as a suggested friend. I dismissed him because I had met him in the past, and there was something about his demeanor that didn't sit well with me. He had never done anything to me, but my "gut" told me to stay away. It finally hit me; he reminded me of someone who had hurt me in the past.

My subconscious mind was saying, "If it looks like a duck, sounds like a duck, it's probably a duck." Basically, I prejudged this man as being exactly like the person who hurt me. I would run into him at local networking meetings and quietly walk away. I never initiated or followed through on any interaction. In my mind, he was a "duck." I chose to ignore his existence. Stuck in my home with only online social media, this man kept showing up in my feed. It was obnoxious how often, despite my attempts to ignore him, social media continued to suggest him as a connection. Then, I began to see his posts through my friend's comments. What in the world is going on?

I continued to ignore this man as I persisted in my self-discovery work. I had successfully battled all my phobias and insecurities, with the exception of one, the man who reminded me of someone who hurt me.

That day, I went onto my computer, and again, his face popped up. Logic told me that I conquered all the other roadblocks in my life, and I will hopefully never meet the person who hurt me again. The best way to beat this fear was to approach it directly. That faithful morning, I wrestled with my fears to simply send a connection request to this man I didn't care to know. He immediately accepted. My insides turned.

What had I done? I may have just allowed my greatest fear back into my life. I watched his profile for a week. I scanned his old posts. Nothing vulgar. Nothing mean. Not anything like I expected him to be. We had hundreds of mutual friends. How bad can he be? My imagination had made him an older version of the person I knew from college. I expected to connect virtually with him and see validation of all my fears, but I didn't see any negative evidence.

I realized that I was still afraid. To overcome this fear, I must do something more. I needed to speak to him. I sent him a private message to start a conversation. We saw humor in the same things. We both had a very practical view of all the chaos that was surrounding the world during the worldwide lockdown. Could I be that wrong about a person? I truly pride myself on my gut instincts. I needed to take a bolder step.

I invited myself over to his front porch for a beer. Keep in mind, this is during the full COVID-19 lockdown with all the social distancing. I breached two stomach-wrenching dangers at once: one, COVID and, two, him.

As I walked up to his porch, he had a selection of beers for me to choose from. We sat socially distanced on his porch, drinking beers as we had discussion after discussion. He was nothing like my imagination created him to be. He was a good-humored man with deep thoughts. Even when we disagreed, it was fun to play verbal volleyball with him.

As the weeks passed, our chairs moved closer together. He became a good friend. One day, I decided to tell him why I avoided him for the eighteen years prior. He was horrified that he had caused me so much anxiety. I apologized for judging him by his look, mannerisms, voice and choice of cars. His personality and mind is nothing of what I feared. Years have now passed. We have created a podcast together called Denim and Pearls—business casual with pearls of wisdom from the porch… where our friendship started.

My lessons learned through the development of our friendship:

1. My "gut instinct"/subconscious mind was marred by my past. I had a list of physical qualities in my mind that I had learned were dangerous. My conscious mind kept seeing him over the years, but I subconsciously avoided him.

2. I had to step toward what I irrationally feared.

3. Don't judge a book by its cover.

If I allowed my subconscious mind to rationally keep me hostage in fear, I would have never met Brian Swanson. He has helped me numerous times through his ability to see life through a different lens. My conscious mind was so quiet. It nudged me gradually to see past what my subconscious refused to permit.

My request to you is to challenge your beliefs every once in a while. Is there someone you keep running into that you are weary of for no reason to speak with? Step out of your comfort zone. Start a conversation.

You never know what your marred subconsciousness is keeping you from discovering. Perhaps you are missing out on your next level of friendship. It could also be affecting your business. Perhaps you are avoiding changes, people, or potentials based on a previous bad experience. Logic it out and move on.

"Your friends will know you better in the first minute you meet than your acquaintances will know you in a thousand years."
~ Richard Bach

MICHELLE MRAS

About Michelle Mras, PhD: Michelle is a Global Award-Winning Keynote & TEDx Speaker, Presentation Coach, co-Host of two podcasts: Denim & Pearls and Amplifluence. Michelle is the Host of MentalShift on The New Channel (TNC), Philippines. She's a multiple Bestselling Author and co-Founder of Amplifuence: Amplifying the influence of Coaches, Authors and Speakers.

Michelle is a survivor of multiple life challenges to include a Traumatic Brain Injury and Breast Cancer. She guides others to recognize the innate gifts within them, stop apologizing for what they are not and step into who they truly are... Unapologetically.

Author's Website: *www.MichelleMras.com*

Book Series Website: *www.The13StepsToRiches.com*

Mickey Stewart

POSTCARDS FROM PERTH

While driving along the River Tay in the city of Perth, Scotland, my husband, Mark, and I stopped at a particular set of lights when suddenly, I had a massive realization that felt like a physical pressure in my chest. I recognized a pattern that preceded all of the biggest and best decisions I ever made in my life.

One of those BIG and BEST decisions was made almost thirty years prior when I found myself just beyond this exact set of lights. Although I didn't call it the sixth sense back then, I had come to recognize the difference between a random thought and a thought 'spark.'

While stopped at the red light, I experienced a momentary flashback to the summer of 1994 when I traveled 2,600 miles across the world from Canada to Scotland and found myself sitting in a pub just a few blocks up the street. As we waited for our clothes to dry at a local laundromat, my friends and I headed across the street to enjoy a pint of beer and to write postcards to our families.

We were tired from traveling and partying the night before, and the buzz from our half-drunk beer had started to kick in. We laughed so much it hurt. As I caught my breath, wiped the laughing tears from my face, and let out a sigh, I told my friends, "I could totally live here."

The words came out of my mouth before I even thought them, but I meant them.

Have you ever had a moment when you've been struck with an intuitive nudge—a Knowing, a thought 'spark'—a strong gut feeling of "this is where I belong" or "this feels RIGHT?" It felt like that. And while my story reflects a PLACE of belonging, your story could represent a product idea, a relationship, or your purpose.

Having had some previous experience with not only listening to but following and trusting my intuitive feelings, I noticed that doing so usually worked out in my favor.

So, five months later, I moved to Scotland; it all stemmed from this one thought that came to me without consciously thinking about it.

Napoleon Hill called the Sixth Sense, *The Door to the Temple of Wisdom*. When you get an intuitive nudge, that door cracks open, and you grab a glimpse of what's inside. Once you see it, you cannot un-see it or forget it. This momentary flash of your potential future feels like being in the foyer of a concert hall that you have never been in.

While waiting to be let into the main auditorium, a cleaner comes through the doors—giving you a quick view of the interior seating and stage. As the doors close behind them, you do not wonder if the auditorium will look the same when they re-open because you have already seen inside.

The Sixth Sense is our intuition. Hill described it as a way "through which Infinite Intelligence may and will communicate voluntarily, without any effort from or demands by the individual." We can't hack or manipulate our intuition, but I have found particular ways to activate it and converse with it.

So, how do we do that? How do we activate and converse with our sixth sense? How can we tell the difference between all the random thoughts and a thought "spark?" An intuitive idea or impulse is accompanied by a Knowing, a strong feeling that comes with its own luggage tag of sorts.

This "tag" is like the neon orange label that helps me recognize my black suitcase on the airport carousel among all the other similar-looking black cases. Those instinctual nudges will feel that obvious to you—bright and bold, with your name written all over them.

The pattern I mentioned that preceded key moments in my life where I felt guided was a three-part pattern. It involved first, the recognition of those gut feelings; second, having the faith to listen to them and not brush them off like a piece of lint; and third, having the courage to decide to act on them.

We can all tap into our sixth sense, but many of us ignore intuition because perhaps we were told as children to be realistic, stop daydreaming, or not be foolish. Well-meaning adults may have encouraged us to do what they thought was best for us, but here's the kicker—we all have a different purpose in life.

What might seem illogical, impulsive, and irrational to someone else may feel like the most natural decision for you. Deciding to move not only to a different country but a different continent, where you only know a handful of people, you have no savings and no backup plan— even I have to admit that sounds like *all kinds of cray-cray*. But I did it anyway. Why? Because even at the age of twenty-three, I had collected enough evidence that trusting my gut led to awesome adventures.

Although I would be as bold to say that, for the most part, having the ability to recognize, listen to, and act on my intuitive nudges is one of my superpowers, sometimes I lose my touch. Sometimes, that *Door to the Temple of Wisdom* locks me out. But just like every door, there must also be a key that unlocks it, like the key to your metaphorical carry-on bag that opens your aptly labeled suitcase of intuitive ideas. For me, that key is gratitude.

Gratitude sounds almost too simple. But that's the beauty of it. Sometimes, it just takes one day of writing in my gratitude journal to shift things. This is one of the ways I communicate with Infinite Intelligence to let it know I am in a state of being that is worthy of and can be trusted with all the goodies it has at the ready.

Taking ink to paper, expressing how happy and grateful I already am, announces, "I'm here to serve. I have good intentions. Come play through me." You become a Transceiver, meaning you can receive messages via your intuition and also transmit messages through your vibration of gratitude. This is Co-Creation with Infinite Intelligence, and it's a fun way to live life.

The simple pleasure of traveling with friends and the memory of laughing at the silliest of things in that pub is one of my favorite pockets of time. When writing those postcards, I was in a state of immense bliss. I distinctly remember imagining Mum receiving hers in the post, saying, "Oh my gosh. How does Mickey expect me to read that? The print is so small," but I was trying to cram as much as possible onto that tiny card.

The eagerness to tell Mum and Dad about all my amazing adventures, coupled with deep gratitude for the experience and the immense joy and laughter I was sharing with my friends—*that* is when the inspired urge (my thought "spark") came to me.

Being guided to move to Scotland wasn't just about the place—it was also about being attracted to the person who lived there who would complement me and my life. Mark's personality, support, and talent have helped me to create my own legacy gifts, follow my interests, and not just listen to my longings but act on them and make a difference in the world. In a way, he also is a key to my lock, as I am the key to his. I could not imagine doing life without him.

When you look back at the biggest and best decisions you made in your lifetime, I suspect you would notice a similar pattern in spotting the thought "sparks" that have your name written all over them, that match the key to your carry-on:

1.   Recognition

2.   Faith to Listen

3.   Courage to Decide

"Have courage to follow your heart and intuition.
They somehow know what you truly want to become."
~ Steve Jobs

MICKEY STEWART

About Mickey Stewart: Born in Cape Breton, Canada, Mickey Stewart is a musician, coach, and author who has been a player and instructor of the snare drum and bodhrán for forty years.

Responsible for heading up the drum program at Ardvreck School in Perthshire, Scotland, since 2002, Mickey is in high demand to teach throughout the U.K. and North America.

Creator and founder of BodhránExpert.com, her YouTube videos have received more than two million views from students and fans from every country throughout the world.

Over the past eight years, she's been involved in the TV and film industry as a supporting artist. Even more recently, she's begun following her newest passion, which is teaching others how to share their talents with the world.

Stewart lives in Crieff, Scotland, with her husband of twenty-six years, Scottish musician and composer Mark Stewart, along with their eighteen-year-old son, Cameron, who is also a piper.

Author's Website: *www.MickeyStewart.com*

Book Series Website: *www.The13StepsToRiches.com*

Mike Green

EMBRACING THE SIXTH SENSE WITH PMA

As I sit down to conclude this book, I'm awed by the journey I've traveled, one marked by twists, turns, and profound realizations. At the heart of it all lies the principle of the sixth sense, a guiding force that has shaped my life in ways I could have never imagined or dreamed.

From the sun-kissed shores of Mission Beach in San Diego, California, where I grew up, where my journey began as a troubled youth, to the tranquil landscapes of North Idaho, where I now find solace with my beloved family, the sixth sense has been my constant companion, leading me through the highs and lows of life.

For me, the sixth sense is more than just a concept; it's a divine channel of communication with God Himself. It's the subtle whispers of intuition, the flashes of insight, and the gentle nudges that guide me along my path, offering clarity and direction when I need it most, guiding me as I put Him first.

My journey with the sixth sense began with a simple prayer uttered amidst the chaos of my teenage years in Juvenal Hall. In those moments of darkness, I reached out to the divine (God), seeking guidance and understanding. In response, the sixth sense revealed itself to me.

When I got out of jail, my dad sat me in the car and asked, "Mike, what do you want to do with your life?" I said, "I don't know, Dad, but I never want to come back here again (and never did)." So, he put a tape in the cassette player from Nightingale Conant's *Psychology of Winning* by Dr. Denis Waitley.

Waitley said, "There are two primary choices in life: to accept conditions as they exist or accept the responsibility for changing them." That was a deciding point in my life, where the Six Senses (God/Divine Providence) showed up and showed me how to take responsibility for my life and to dream bigger. That prayer was answered, and as I continued, I became a student of success.

I visualized success and prayed that God would give me hope and a vision of my future. Napoleon Hill became my mentor at 14. As I stole tapes from my dad and then bought them later, my favorite became *Science of Personal Achievement* by Napoleon Hill. His childhood was a lot like mine.

God would have it now, as I am an instructor with the Napoleon Hill Foundation for the same program, but now it's called the Science of Success, The PMA Program. My friends are people like the CEO of the Napoleon Hill Foundation, Don Green. He has adopted me as his nephew, and I call him Uncle. Denis Waitley, who spoke into my life through his audiobook tapes, who was my Jiminy Cricket, guided me into thinking right and led me to the Psychology of Success. It is no coincidence—it is Divine Providence that brought me here with the sixth sense.

God is a beacon of hope in the midst of uncertainty; we just have to cry out to him or just sit with him and ask.

To clarify the meaning of the sixth sense through my experiences in life, another defining moment stands out—a moment of clarity and revelation during a speaking engagement at Erik Swanson's Habitude Warrior Conference in Dallas, Texas.

I was seeking to change my speeches, and Erik said, "Think of three things." I thought of PMA and its true meaning through the sixth sense, so as I was floating on my back in the pool asking God through the sixth sense, pondering the true meaning of PMA, I heard a voice within asking me, "How do you talk to me?"

At that moment, I realized the power of prayer. I said, "PRAYER! THAT'S HOW I TALK TO YOU!" God spoke again, asking, "And how do I talk to you?" I replied, "Through meditation and being still, and with visions: desire and inspiration through my imagination."

It was a realization like it was a radio transmitter/receiver. Hill talks about channels to the divine through communication with the Maker of Heaven and Earth and everything in it, the Maker of the Universe itself. There it was—the formula for success laid before me. Prayer, meditation, through the inspiration of a burning desire, bringing you to Definite Major Purpose through this sixth sense and imagination.

It all ties together in life and success. Lastly, as I was still floating on my back, God asked through the sixth sense, "What do you do with the visions, desires, and inspiration or hunches that come through the sixth sense?" With amazing excitement, I responded, "Action, massive ACTION." Yes, action! There it is, the "A" in PMA.

There it was, the formula to success in its simplest form I have ever SEEN. PMA is the key to unlocking the power of the sixth sense and your future. And so, I embraced the formula for success:

$$P + M + A = PMA$$

It always starts within with PRAYER, then MEDITATION (listening and receiving), and ACTION.

The force of following through with that inspiration and knowing in your spirit the guidance that you were given is a transmitting and receiving set that we all have; we just have to use it. The result is a Positive Mental Attitude. The Gratitude Attitude with a Burning Desire—the foundation upon which all great achievements are built.

As I bid farewell to this chapter, "The Sixth Sense," which was, at first, honestly overwhelming. But I love and understand with revelation, and I invite you to embrace the sixth sense as the 13th principle of success. Trust in the divine guidance that flows through you, and let it be your guiding light through life's challenges and triumphs. With faith, intuition, and a clear vision of your purpose, there's no limit to what you can achieve.

May your journey be filled with blessings, and may the sixth sense illuminate your path to greatness. God bless. PMA ALL THE WAY.

MIKE GREEN

About Mike Green: Mike Green has been a lifelong student of Napoleon Hill. Napoleon Hill's philosophy profoundly impacted Green as a teenager, giving him the tools to structure his thinking in a way that allowed him to design and achieve his dreams. From a delinquent beach rat to living his destiny, Mike transformed his life, pursuing passions like acting, bodybuilding, speaking, and ultimately attracting his soulmate. He won the Pacific USA Teenage Championships, became a commercial actor and model, and met the girl of his dreams, who has been his wife for over thirty-five years.

Mike now resides in Idaho with his family of five beautiful children in the mountains of God's Country. Over the years, he has helped many young people with this philosophy. As a juvenile detention officer and mentor, Green worked closely with kids, inspiring and guiding them. Today, he operates a private gym, Muscle Mike's Gym, where he continues to train and mentor kids, both physically and mentally.

A graduate of the Napoleon Hill Foundation and an instructor and speaker/trainer of the PMA Science of Success, Mike speaks nationally and internationally. He is also a realtor, real estate investor, and coach in North Idaho.

Mike's philosophy is rooted in giving to live—by inspiring others to pursue their dreams and desires while promoting a culture of helping others with a hand up, encouragement, and love. His mission is to inspire, serve, and uplift others. God bless.

Author's Website: *www.CDAMike.com*

Book Series Website: *www.The13StepsToRiches.com*

Natalie Susi

THE MAGIC OF YOUR MIND

As you open your mind to the possibilities of the universe, you begin to realize that there is more to life than what meets the eye. You start to understand that there is a sixth sense that is within us all, waiting to be unlocked and harnessed. This sixth sense is the key to connecting one's mind with the universe's mind, and it holds the power to transmute desires into material form. So, let us explore the power of the sixth sense and how it can be harnessed to unlock the door to the temple of wisdom through meditation and the power of the Creative Imagination.

This principle is the apex of philosophy and can only be understood and applied after mastering the other twelve principles. The sixth sense is the portion of the subconscious mind referred to as the Creative Imagination, and it is the "receiving set" through which ideas, plans, and thoughts flash into the mind. The sixth sense is probably the medium of contact between the finite mind of man and Infinite Intelligence. It is a mixture of both the mental and the spiritual and can be induced to aid in transmuting desires into concrete or material form.

I cannot emphasize enough the importance of the sixth sense. It is the key to connecting our minds with the universe's mind, and it is the ultimate power of connection. For years, I dedicated countless hours to perfecting the art of meditation, and through this, I gained control over my mind. However, perfection can never be fulfilled, but day by day, you will see the improvement in your life and spiritual well-being. My sixth sense has unlocked doors that I never knew were possible.

It has enhanced my outlook on the world and given me a sense of peace among the hardships of life. The benefits were immense—new opportunities and blessings poured into my life, and I gained a deeper understanding of myself and my purpose in this world. I truly believe that the sixth sense is the pinnacle of the philosophy of the twelve principles, and it can only be understood and applied once the other principles are mastered. It is a mixture of both the mental and the spiritual, and with its aid, we can transmute our desires into material form.

To truly understand the sixth sense, one needs to develop their mind from within through meditation. This power is believed to be the point at which the mind of man contacts the Universal Mind. It is the First Cause, or Intelligence, which permeates every atom of matter and embraces every unit of energy perceptible to man. By emulating the great feeling and acting as nearly as possible, one can become truly great.

For example, many successful entrepreneurs use their creative imagination to envision their goals and turn them into reality. They use their sixth sense to receive ideas, plans, and thoughts that can help them manifest their dreams. Through meditation and the development of the sixth sense, we can tap into this powerful tool and use it to achieve our own goals and aspirations.

After working for several years in a successful product business, I was still left unfulfilled and unsatisfied. It took me a long time to face the realization that my business, Bare Mixers, was not in alignment with my purpose and calling. This is a scary realization to face since I dedicated countless hours, money, and my freedom to make this business a success. Starting over is even scarier, leaving behind a successful venture in hopes of pursuing another one.

However, by tapping into my sixth sense day in and day out, I realized my true calling: becoming a holistic communication coach. My sixth sense is what gave me the courage to walk away from Bare Mixers and restart my career. Your sixth sense needs to be your best friend, and you need to pour effort and patience into it so you can receive all the desires that are placed on your heart.

Another powerful aspect of harnessing the sixth sense is through the practice of holding council meetings with "Invisible Counselors." This unique technique involves engaging in nightly sessions where we imagine and interact with imaginary figures who possess the traits of character we aspire to acquire. During these meetings, our "Invisible Counselors" become, in a sense, real and tangible. We can call upon them for guidance and wisdom.

Let me provide an example to illustrate the impact of this practice:

Imagine being in a council meeting, seated at the table with your Invisible Counselors. As you close your eyes and delve into the depths of your creative imagination, you invite Thomas Edison to join the gathering.

In your mind's eye, you see him walk over and take a seat to your left. With great anticipation, you seek Edison's insight on the path you should take. To your astonishment, he leans forward and shares, "You are destined to witness the discovery of the secret of life." These words reverberate within you, igniting a spark of inspiration and purpose. In that moment, you realize the profound impact this practice can have on your character development and personal growth. By engaging with these Invisible Counselors, you tap into their collective wisdom and knowledge, transcending the limitations of time and space.

Through this extraordinary technique, your mind becomes a gateway to a realm where past luminaries and visionaries can guide you on your journey. The Invisible Counselors offer invaluable perspectives and ideas that can reshape your thinking and pave the way for personal transformation. By embracing the practice of holding council meetings with these Invisible Counselors, you tap into the vast reservoir of wisdom and inspiration that exists within your own mind. This empowers you to rebuild your character, gain clarity on your purpose, and unlock the doors to your fullest potential.

Remember, the sixth sense and the practice of engaging with Invisible Counselors are not mere fantasies. They are tools that bridge the gap between your conscious and subconscious mind, allowing you to access deeper levels of creativity and intuition. With dedication and belief in this process, you can harness the power of your mind to manifest extraordinary results in your life.

In conclusion, the journey towards harnessing the power of the sixth sense requires a solid foundation built upon the mastery of the twelve principles that precede it. Each principle serves as a steppingstone, providing the necessary groundwork to fully comprehend and apply the immense potential of the sixth sense. The sixth sense acts as a catalyst, a force that propels us forward in the transmutation of our desires into tangible reality. It serves as the bridge between the realms of the mental and the spiritual, enabling us to tap into the infinite intelligence that permeates the universe.

In essence, by mastering the twelve principles, developing the mind through meditation, and engaging in imaginary council meetings with "Invisible Counselors," we unlock the door to the temple of wisdom. We transcend limitations, manifest our desires, and align ourselves with the infinite intelligence of the universe. Embracing the power of the sixth sense, we embark on a transformative journey that leads us to a profound understanding of ourselves and our purpose in this world.

NATALIE SUSI

About Natalie Susi: Natalie has more than fourteen years of experience as a teacher, speaker, entrepreneur, and mentor. Currently, she's a six-year UCSD professor focusing on communications and the Pursuit of Happiness. As an entrepreneur, she founded and grew Bare Organic Mixers beverage company for eight years, resulting in an acquisition in 2014.

After selling the company, Natalie combined her educational background as a teacher and her experience as an entrepreneur to provide personal development coaching and consulting to individuals, businesses, and creative entrepreneurs. She developed a program called Conscious Conversations and utilizes a step-by-step process called The Alignment Method to support leaders in cultivating conscious teams and businesses through a process of self-reflection, self-discovery, and self-ascension that ultimately increases profits, productivity, and the growth of the individuals, personally and professionally.

Author's Website: *www.NatalieSusi.com*

Book Series Website: *www.The13StepsToRiches.com*

Nita Patel

TRUSTING INTUITION

Your Inner Guide to Success

We live in a world where information is at our fingertips, data drives decisions, and logical reasoning is often regarded as the highest form of intelligence. Yet, there's a more subtle, often overlooked form of guidance that plays a powerful role in achieving success: intuition. You may have heard of it described as a "gut feeling," "inner voice," or "sixth sense."

Intuition, though intangible, can be a compass that directs us toward choices aligned with our deepest values and purpose. When nurtured and trusted, intuition can lead to remarkable outcomes in both personal and professional realms. This chapter delves into what intuition truly is, why it's essential to success, and how trusting it can transform one's life.

What is Intuition?

Intuition is the ability to understand or sense something instinctively without the need for conscious reasoning. Think of it as a form of intelligence that bypasses the logical mind and taps into a well of accumulated experiences, emotions, and subconscious knowledge. Intuition isn't magical or unexplainable; instead, it's the brain's way of quickly synthesizing vast amounts of information that might be hard to process in real-time.

Research shows that intuition is often informed by subconscious cues we've picked up from past experiences, patterns we've noticed, and knowledge we've absorbed over time. The mind is like a data processor, sorting through these bits of information in milliseconds to produce what we experience as an "intuition." By drawing on past knowledge and experience, intuition gives us an edge in complex or uncertain situations, offering an almost immediate, holistic perspective that rational thinking may not arrive at so quickly.

Why Intuition is Essential for Success

Success often hinges on making the right decision at the right time. It's not just about having the correct data or following conventional wisdom; it's about reading between the lines, seeing potential where others might not, and having the courage to take risks. Here's why intuition is an invaluable tool on the path to success:

1. **Clarity in Ambiguity**: When information is incomplete or unclear, relying solely on logic can create analysis paralysis. Intuition cuts through the fog, offering a sense of clarity that allows us to act even when facts are limited.

2. **Authenticity & Alignment**: Intuition guides us towards choices that resonate with our true selves, fostering authenticity in decision-making. When we act in alignment with our inner values and beliefs, we are more likely to attract opportunities and relationships that align with our goals.

3. **Enhanced Creativity & Problem-Solving**: Intuition is a creative force, as it draws on seemingly unrelated information to inspire solutions that aren't always obvious. It allows us to see connections between ideas that a strictly logical approach might miss, promoting innovative thinking.

4. **Faster Decision-Making**: Quick decisions are essential in fast-paced situations. Since intuition operates almost instantaneously, it enables us to make swift choices without needing to analyze every variable. This speed can be a game-changer, particularly in high-stakes environments.

Recognizing & Honing Intuition

While intuition is a natural human trait, it often goes unrecognized or unused. Trusting your intuition is a skill that grows with practice and awareness. Here are a few strategies to develop and strengthen this skill:

1. **Listen to Your Body:** The body is often the first to respond to intuition. When faced with a decision, pay attention to physical sensations—a tightening in the stomach, a quickened heartbeat, or a sense of ease. These can be clues as to whether something is right or wrong for you.

2. **Practice Mindfulness:** Mindfulness practices, like meditation, help quiet the mind and tune out external noise, making it easier to recognize intuitive signals. With a calm mind, you can hear that "inner voice" more clearly and separate it from fear or anxiety-driven thoughts.

3. **Reflect on Past Experiences:** Reflecting on situations where you followed your intuition (or ignored it) can be enlightening. Analyzing these experiences can help you understand how your intuition communicates with you and build confidence in trusting it.

4. **Journal Regularly:** Journaling helps process emotions and experiences, which can strengthen your intuitive sense over time. Writing down your thoughts can bring buried feelings or insights to the surface, allowing you to spot patterns in your thinking and gut reactions.

5. **Start Small:** If trusting your intuition doesn't come naturally, start with small, low-stakes decisions. Let it guide you on simple choices, like what book to read next or which route to take home. As you see positive results from these smaller choices, you'll feel more confident using your intuition for bigger decisions.

Steve Jobs once said, "Have the courage to follow your heart and intuition. They somehow already know what you truly want to become."

Jobs frequently leaned on intuition to guide his decisions at Apple, from product design to business strategy. His ability to foresee trends and create groundbreaking products came not only from logic but also from his gut feelings about what people needed and wanted.

Overcoming Doubts & External Opinions

Trusting intuition doesn't always mean making decisions that others will understand or agree with. Success requires courage, especially when your inner voice leads you down an unconventional path. In these situations, it's essential to stay true to yourself and remember that your intuition is based on your unique experiences, values, and understanding of the world.

While it's important to consider advice from mentors, family, and friends, remember that they can only offer perspectives based on their own experiences, biases, and fears. Your intuition, however, is personalized and rooted in who you are and what you aspire to be. Learning to trust it over others' opinions can be empowering and freeing, building the confidence needed to pursue your dreams and goals with authenticity.

Balancing Intuition with Rational Thought

Trusting intuition doesn't mean ignoring logic. In fact, some of the best decisions are made by balancing both. Logic provides structure, ensuring you're realistic and informed, while intuition offers insight and authenticity. The combination can be incredibly powerful.

Consider intuition a guide that leads you to choices aligned with your deeper self and rational thought and a way to implement those choices wisely. For example, suppose you feel intuitively drawn to a specific career change. In that case, it's wise to use logical reasoning to plan out the transition—researching the industry, networking, and evaluating financial stability. When intuition and logic work together, they create a powerful synergy that supports both inspired and grounded action.

Building a Relationship with Your Intuition

Ultimately, trusting your intuition is about building a relationship with yourself. Just as you would cultivate a friendship, building trust with your inner voice requires patience, consistency, and open-mindedness. The more you listen, the stronger your intuition will become.

Here are some daily practices that can help you foster this relationship:

- **Daily Check-Ins**: Spend a few minutes each day simply observing how you feel. Without judgment or analysis, acknowledge what your body and mind are telling you. Over time, this habit will make it easier to recognize intuitive messages.

- **Affirmations for Trust**: Using affirmations like "I trust my inner guidance" or "My intuition leads me to success" can help reinforce your confidence in this subtle guidance.

- **Celebrate Successes**: Celebrate every time you trust your intuition, and it leads to a positive outcome. Consider these successes affirmations of your inner wisdom.

Trusting your intuition is not about taking shortcuts or hoping for magic; it's about honoring the deeper parts of yourself and allowing them to guide you toward choices that feel right. Intuition is a skill, a gift, and a practice. The more you trust it, the more you become in tune with your true purpose and the path to success that feels most genuine.

By embracing your intuition, you open yourself up to a new level of potential and possibility. Each time you let it lead, you build a stronger foundation for success that isn't solely reliant on external validation or conventional metrics but grounded in self-trust, authenticity, and resilience. Let your intuition be the compass that guides you to a life that is not only successful but deeply fulfilling.

NITA PATEL

About Nita Patel: Nita Patel is an artist, author, and executive coach with the mission of Healing the World Through Art. Her vibrant abstract paintings and mixed-media pieces have graced prestigious galleries worldwide, including the Louvre in Paris.

After her studies at Harvard in Industrial-Organizational Psychology, she blended her passion and profession, integrating creative expression with workplace wellness. With over two decades of experience in technology and business leadership roles, she now shares inspiration and transformation through her art, art therapy workshops, and executive coaching services.

Author's Website: *www.Nita-Patel.com*

Book Series Website: *www.The13StepsToRiches.com*

Olga Geidane

WHO IS TALKING TO ME?

Some call it a sixth sense; others refer to it as a gut feeling; many say it is intuition, and a few will do their best to prove it's your higher self and divine wisdom.

Ultimately, no one doubts its existence; however, people fight over the name of it. And who cares?

I refer to it as my intuition. If you choose to call it something else, let's respect each other's views and move on to the most important part: how can we use that to help us succeed in life, business, and relationships?

And just in case you think you have none of it, let me ask you a few questions.

Have you been in a situation where you left home and something inside of you told you to take an umbrella or another item, and later in the day, you were like, "Oh, that's great. I took it despite no logic of carrying this with me!"

Or perhaps you call someone out of a blue moon, and they say they were literally thinking of you?

Or you met someone and, instantly, for no apparent reason, you just… don't click with that person, and you just don't like them? And then later on, you find out they actually are a bit of a nutter and have a history of hurting people one way or another?

Or did you make a decision based on "it felt good," and it happened to be the best decision ever?

So... all of this is precisely that: the sixth sense, gut feeling, intuition, your higher self, divine wisdom, or anything else you wish to call it.

The fact you haven't made friends with it yet and haven't collaborated so far doesn't mean it is not there. Everyone has it. But not everyone listens to it. Why? Because not everyone is aware of the hidden power of it. And let's admit it, it's not something you would learn at school or college, so it remains a secret to so many and a powerful tool to a few.

Today, I would like to introduce you to how you can collaborate with your sixth sense in order to skyrocket your life.

Start Listening to the Whispers of Your Inner Voice

To be able to collaborate with your intuition, you have to learn how to *listen*. If you are already great at that, feel free to skip this part.

Believe me or not, this is the hardest part for so many people. The reason for it is your distractions and the number of thoughts you have in your head on a permanent basis. Start practicing quieting your mind. Whether you do it through meditation, walking in nature, journaling, or anything else, it is entirely up to you. The idea is to calm your mind and get the chaos out so you can start hearing the whispering of your sixth sense.

And why do I keep mentioning whispering? Well, because this is how it will feel in the beginning. I haven't met anyone going from no internal messaging at all to full-on channeling and receiving life-changing information. There will be small, often even insignificant messages in the beginning, and the more you listen to them and, most importantly, follow up on them, the louder that voice will get, and you will receive even stronger messages!

One of my clients once said to me, "Olga, I decided I will just play a game with my intuition—so every time I get a message, I score a point, and then every day, I count how many I have." Whether you play such games or not, it's up to you. What matters most is you listening to the inner guidance that very often comes as an inside message, something like, "call X-Y-Z person," or a nudge—a big desire, or a feeling to do something right away or at the earliest convenience.

Follow the Guidance of Your Sixth Sense

What's the point of having any step-by-step guidance or a manual? To get you to the outcome, end goal, or target. The same applies to your internal messaging. It is the ultimate wisdom that knows all the shortcuts and best ways to get you to where you need to be.

By the way, yes—it is about where you need to be, not necessarily where you want to end up! But the good news is that you would never *want* to be somewhere and do something without having that experience as part of your purpose, which ultimately means you need it.

Just try and see what happens when you do every tiny thing your inner self tells you to do. You will notice a massive increase in alignment with everything and everyone around you because everything is connected. We just can't see the connection behind all those distractions we are surrounded by on a daily basis.

When the first lockdown in the UK (and the rest of the world) was announced, all business owners were told to close their businesses for a few months with a promise that it would be only for a few months. My inner voice screamed inside of me to shut down my office completely.

And here is the thing: these messages often come in an order, without explanations, so even when you want to know more—you can't! All you do is just follow it.

Without knowing anything else about the future, I decided to follow my intuition and gave notice to my landlord, who tried to talk me out of it. I was insistent and even referred to my intuition as the reason—as you can imagine, he laughed and said that the government promised we would be back in the game in the next few months... You know already the rest of the story. I am just so happy that the step of shutting down my in-person office completely ultimately led me to my dream lifestyle: traveling worldwide without being attached to one location. And that was my dream for decades!

Trust Your Intuition 100% & Never Doubt it, Even When Your Logic Disagrees

What if I tell you that your intuition is your best friend, best consultant and advisor, and it is NEVER WRONG?

The other day, I lost my earring in Podgorica, Montenegro. I was very upset because it was custom-made and purchased on the island of La Gomera, Canary Islands. My intuition told me I would find it, so together with my husband, we walked all the way to the places we were the day before. I went through the entire hotel room, and it was nowhere; we asked at reception if anyone found and delivered an earring to them, which was not the case. I was very sad when we had to leave Montenegro the next day because I knew that all the chances of finding my lost earring would drop to zero.

A week later, when we were packing for another trip from Stockholm to Gothenburg, I was going through my clothing on the hangers and found it attached to one of them. I screamed out loud—that's how happy I was and instantly apologized to myself for not trusting my intuition.

You will be in a situation of doubt; your logic will tell it this is not the right move, but just trust your sixth sense. Just believe and know it is always, always, always right.

So, next time you receive a message, don't doubt it; just do it.

Ask Simple Questions

As you have practiced careful listening, following the guidance, and trusting 100%, your gut feeling will become stronger or you will hear it louder. Is it one or the other—who cares? The most important thing is that you are now ready to collaborate on anything you want in life.

For that, start asking simple questions internally or in writing, if that's easier for you. For example, "Should I say yes to this deal?" or "Shall I purchase this?" or "Shall I go on a date with this person?"

Please remember not to trick yourself into the opposite, desired answer. If you get a strong yes—that's a yes. If you get a "no" or doubt—that's a no. Remember, doubt means a "no"—you just don't know the real and logical reason yet.

It's so easy to think yourself into what you want and to end up regretting not listening to your intuition. Avoid asking complicated questions, something like, "Is this job I am offered good for me and will help me with my career?" and instead ask, "Should I take this job?"

Practice. Practice. Practice.

Imagine learning a brand-new language. How long will it take you before you will be able to speak it fluently?

You see, the same applies to the sixth sense. It is not natural for an adult to suddenly start listening to inner guidance. But the more you practice, the better you will become. Just trust and have faith in this process.

I wish you all the best on this journey of discovering and collaborating with your intuition! This is, for sure, the best and the easiest way of living our lives!

I look forward to learning more about your journey with intuition and sixth sense! If you have any questions or would like to share a success story, feel free to email me: Olga@newlifekickstart.com.

OLGA GEIDANE

Olga is an International Speaker, an Event MC/Host, a Facilitator, a Mindset Coach, a Bestselling Author, and a Regional President of the Professional Speaking Association in the UK. She is a host of Olga's Show and A World-Traveler.

Olga helps ambitious people to unlock their extraordinary performance and their true, authentic side. She is passionate about helping people to live their best lives.

Olga knows how tough it is to be broke and unfulfilled in life: At the age of twenty-four, just after her divorce, Olga came to the UK from Latvia with no spoken English, with just £100 in her pocket, and a two-year-old son. Olga is a very inspirational survivor: She went through abuse, betrayal, cheating, financial loss, and emotional breakdown.

Matt Black (Business Model Innovation & Disruption Consultant—Snr. Advisor to CEO CSO CCO COO—Author & International Public Speaker) said: "Olga really takes it up a notch beyond anything I have seen before. She is one of the bravest people I have ever seen on stage. If you are looking to book a speaker or attend a talk that will be inspiring, challenging, and leave you wanting to take action... She is perfect."

Author's Website: *www.OlgaGeidane.com*

Book Series Website: *www.The13StepsToRiches.com*

Phillip D. McClure

GRANT ME CHANGE FOR INNER PEACE

The Sixth Sense: A Blend of Mental Faculties

The Sixth Sense Ref. *Think and Grow Rich* is a powerful culmination of our mental faculties working together. It's not just intuition but a blend—a complete integration of the mind's unique functions. When these faculties harmonize, they produce something transformative that leads to true inner peace. It's less about the time it takes or the difficulty and more about reaching a moment, a catalyst that takes you in a new direction.

Finding My Catalytic Journey of Radical Change

I experienced my own catalyst when I reached a point where something felt missing in my life. I was surrounded by (the trappings of) success—good friends, nice cars, museums, and the beauty of Utah. But despite all that, my self-love cup was perpetually empty. I realized I had to make a drastic change to find fulfillment.

In that moment of searching, I turned to my six-year-old son and asked, "Where would you want to live?" He said, "Tennessee." I made the decision on the spot to move, sold all of my possessions, bought a house sight unseen, and left Utah. This move became the start of my inward journey toward finding peace and self-love.

Pruning for Peace: The Power of Letting Go

When you take a step like this, you'll hear people say, "Cut everyone off that doesn't support you." I think of it differently; I call it pruning. When pruning a tree, you allow for healthier growth by creating space for more light to come in. It's not about being harsh to people—it's about creating space to work on yourself. The people who no longer align with your path naturally fall away, leaving room for new growth.

As I continued this journey, something remarkable happened. The projects and individuals I pruned quickly drifted away, and those who were right for me began to appear in my life. It felt like I was going through a natural reintroduction of myself—a reintroduction to a better, more peaceful version of who I had become.

Granting Myself Permission to Grow

An essential part of my growth was learning to grant myself permission —to say "yes" to what I needed without external validation and "no" to the things that were no longer aligned for me. This kind of decision-making can be challenging. Society teaches us to seek permission from everyone else or give it only for what is deemed a worthy goal, yet it rarely tells us to give permission to ourselves for what is best and most aligned for us for what we feel is a worthy goal. The moment I allowed myself to follow my intuition, I could move forward with the next steps of my life freely.

I grounded myself, created my peace, and discovered that granting self-permission is foundational to living authentically. From there, I had the freedom to move from one meaningful choice to another with joy, peace, and without regret.

The Power of Community: A New Direction with YU2SHINE

One of the greatest gifts that came from my journey was finding like-minded people through the YU2SHINE community led by Victoria Rader. I'd planned to take a year off just after I retired, when her CEO, Marla found me and started teaching me wonderful skills. I knew that I had been shown my next chapter. After a year, almost to the day from when I started my journey, Victoria asked if I would step in as CMO for YU2SHINE. I felt a powerful "yes" in my heart. This organization, spanning over seventy countries, has given me opportunities to support others in overcoming negative subconscious patterns and embracing their own journeys toward transformation.

I believe in this work so deeply that I'm thrilled to offer resources, like our free Quantum Leap eBook and the actual proprietary technique that accompanies it. Both are available at MyGiftOffer.com. If you are ready to leave the prison of self-sabotage and truly take the quantum leap to freedom, this gift is for you.

Testimonial Dedication

What you teach allows for a greater capacity to deepen that within yourself. All masters are masters because they are also always learning as a student while seeking to elevate others through teaching. You cannot master anything without also being willing to be a student and a teacher.

To everyone involved in *The 13 Steps to Riches* project, thank you for giving me the platform to share my story. Your guidance and support have not only allowed me to contribute to something meaningful but also expanded my own capacity to receive and give more wisdom. This series has truly enriched my life. To anyone considering this journey—take it with open arms, and let it transform you as it has transformed me.

PHILLIP D. MCCLURE

About Phillip D. McClure: Phillip is a very proud father of two exciting kids and serves his community as a little league football coach. He was raised in the great state of Montana before moving to Mississippi.

Phil lives life to the fullest. His accomplishments consist of completing a full Ironman, retired after twenty-four years in the Army deploying four times and earning multiple decorations along the way—including two Utah crosses! This makes him the only soldier in history to receive that medal twice.

Currently, Phil is the CMO of YU2SHINE and the Owner of NorthStar Coins. It was during his last deployment that he accidentally created his first Mastermind and it has forever changed his life as well as the others involved. He mentors and coaches in FREE mE EFT™ and Theta Healing ® self-improvement and physical fitness.

Phil is an exotic car enthusiast who spends as much time behind the wheel as possible, whether it is carving through canyons, ripping around the racetrack, or coaching others to see their potential. Competitive driving is the best therapy in the world.

Live life to the fullest and have fun while doing it. You don't get a rewind in life so take mistakes as the lessons they are and improve, but don't make the same mistakes twice.

Live in flow, not with the flow.

Authors website: *www.YU2Shine.com* & *www.NorthStarCoins.com*

Book Series Website: *www.The13StepsToRiches.com*

Robyn Kaye Scott

LET'S ALL BE LIKE KEYTON

You are being fooled. You might even feel the trickery, even if you don't know how to describe it. You live in a hyper-connected world through texts, emails, and social media, yet you most likely feel more disconnected than ever.

What was once a last resort—using texts and social media to stay in touch—has now become our primary way of communicating. We likely do this because it's easy, letting us reach so many people in far less time. But what are we sacrificing?

In today's world, we don't need to meet up with people to connect. But that doesn't mean we shouldn't, whenever we can.

Misunderstandings and missed opportunities are common when we communicate through screens. Emojis have become a big part of our interactions just to convey the right tone behind our words. But can an emoji truly express your deep sorrow, true joy, or sincere apology the way your face and voice can? Probably not, and now more than ever, we need to rediscover the lost art of face-to-face, heart-to-heart connection and communication.

Companies are even investing significant resources to teach young people phone skills and conversation techniques because screen communication has diminished our everyday dialogue abilities. While our world is richer for having many ways to connect, we must remember the unmatched power of in-person connection. If you want to be a person of influence, someone capable of inspiring others and fostering real relationships, you need to bring people together.

There is true power in connecting people.

I have spent my life believing in and benefitting from my ability to bring people together, both literally and figuratively. This power blesses lives and enriches souls. It builds businesses and grows organizations.

Some people experience anxiety in groups, withdraw out of fear of rejection, or avoid connection simply because they don't know what to say. But these are opportunities waiting to be captured.

You have a chance to become a better connector and hone your skills in connecting others. Everyone is searching for someone, and few skills are as valuable as the ability to make the introductions that could change lives.

- Introduce yourself
- Introduce others
- Invite people to meet up
- Invite people to connect
- Be a mediator
- Be a problem solver for people
- Create a playground where everyone will want to play

Let's start with the three myths that might be holding you back from more connections and success:

- You don't have to be the life of the party to bring people together.
- You don't have to be an extrovert to start a conversation.
- You don't have to be a "people person" to discover the joy of connecting those who need each other most.

There is a real challenge—a downright problem—with people connecting these days. The good news is that you can be the solution everyone needs, and you'll discover the rewards for doing so.

When we're hosting events, building audiences, networking like pros, and connecting people who care, we become exactly as known and needed as we want to be. In a world where tech can feel overwhelming, your ability to connect will make you invaluable.

Keyton, my son, showed me the beauty of connecting, even in small, simple ways. When he was thirteen, I noticed he'd wave to random people whenever we drove somewhere. One day, I asked him who he was waving at. His answer was simple: "Just people." Curious, I asked, "Why?" Without missing a beat, he shared a story he'd heard.

"There was a man who was so sad in life that he thought his only choice was to end it. He had lost his family, hated his job, and felt that everyone would be better off without him. One day, sitting in traffic, he'd made up his mind to end it all. But then, he looked over at the car next to him and saw a young boy waving at him."

The simple gesture changed the man's perspective. For the first time, he felt truly seen. That small, kind wave saved his life.

Keyton told me, "You just never know who needs to be seen." That moment moved me to my core. I realized Keyton and I share a mission: to bring people together so that no one feels invisible or alone. We all matter, and we all leave a footprint.

The sixth sense we are all called to develop grows from these stories and lessons. By opening ourselves up to the quiet, powerful moments of human connection, we tap into a deeper intuition that guides us to act in ways that unite and uplift others. Like Keyton, we learn that even the simplest actions—a wave, a smile, or a word—can resonate deeply and transform a life.

By practicing compassion and extending kindness to everyone around us, we begin to refine our intuitive senses, developing that sixth sense to understand others and find purpose in serving them. This sixth sense is about recognizing the unseen need, sensing when and where to connect, and using our influence for good.

I am immensely grateful to the creators of *The 13 Steps to Riches* series. This journey has been a remarkable experience, and I'm honored to be a part of it.

To the authors, readers, and everyone who has embraced these teachings, thank you for allowing us to bring these messages of hope, connection, and empowerment to life.

My hope is to help connect people and unite them back into this world through my gifts and methods, and I believe that by following these steps, we can make this world a more connected, compassionate place.

Let's do this! I invite you to CONNECT!

ROBYN KAYE SCOTT

About Robyn Kaye Scott: Robyn Kaye Scott is a Habit Finder Coach and has worked closely with the Og Mandino Group. She is also a certified Master Your Emotions Coach through Inscape World. Robyn Scott is commonly known as the Queen of Connection and Princess of Play in professional communities. She has been working hard for the past nine years to hone her skills as a mentor and coach.

Scott strives to teach people to annihilate judgments, embrace their own stories, and empower themselves to rediscover who they truly are. Scott is an international speaker and also teaches how to present yourself on stage.

Her first book, *Bringing People Together: Rediscovering the Lost Art of Face-to-Face Connecting, Collaborating, and Creating* was released in August 2019 and was a Bestseller in seven categories. Including her own book, Robyn is also a contributing co-author and 17x #1 Bestselling Author in *The 13 Steps To Riches* and *The Book of Influence* by Habitude Warrior and Integrity Publishing International.

Author's Website: *www.RobynKayeScott.com*

Book Series Website: *www.The13StepsToRiches.com*

Dr. Shannon Whittington

KNOW YOUR INNER-SELF

We have all heard about the five senses (sight, sound, smell, taste, and touch), but did you know that each of us has a sixth sense? It's called our intuition, and it often goes unnoticed. Yet, it's arguably the most important of all. According to Merriam-Webster, intuition is "the power or faculty of attaining to direct knowledge or cognition without evident rational thought and inference." Intuition can be our best friend if we put it to work, and doing so can assist us daily. It can help us reach our short-term and long-term goals. So, how do we make our intuition work in our favor?

Meditate

Honing into your sixth sense isn't always the easiest endeavor, but it is possible with a little practice. With so much going on in our day-to-day lives, from work to home and everything in between, we often find ourselves drowning out that still small voice deep inside us.

That's why it's so important to take the time out and spend time listening to it. This can be done in a number of ways. You can spend time alone in the great outdoors, whether at a park or in your backyard, simply sitting and allowing nature to sway you toward your intuition. You can meditate indoors using a meditation app, such as Calm, or play one of the many guided meditation apps on YouTube.

You can seek out guided meditation sessions in person so that you can feel a sense of community and kinship as you work to access your sixth sense. It may not come so easily at first since we have so many racing thoughts about our work tasks, chores, etc., but as long as you work to let those thoughts come and go and redirect your focus to your breathing, you're on the right track.

Exercise

To stay sharp and help you tune in to your intuition, it's not enough to just sit still, you also have to find time to move your wonderful, beautiful body. Exercising releases feel-good brain chemicals, such as dopamine, serotonin, and norepinephrine, all of which can help you become more in tune with your sixth sense.

I imagine that a few of you may be groaning after reading these suggestions. Some of you may not think too much about fitness or meditation, or you may feel that you simply don't have the time with your busy schedules. But with just a few minutes a day, you will be surprised how your intuition will become stronger and stronger as it guides you in the right direction by practicing meditation and exercise.

There are a myriad of workout videos on YouTube at your fingertips targeting every key area of the body; all you have to do is press play. I recommend dedicating at least five days a week to working out (two days of cardio, two days of weight training, and one day of yoga or stretching to keep your muscles guessing), and if dumbbells aren't in your budget, I highly suggest purchasing a set of resistance bands instead. They're affordable and get the job done.

Secondly, I know you're most likely quite busy, but do you have thirty minutes to spare? I'm willing to bet you do. Studies show that thirty minutes of exercise a day works just as well as sessions that last sixty minutes. Getting into a fitness routine may feel daunting at first, and you may not be able to keep up with the people guiding your workouts, but all you have to do is show up and give it your all. Your intuition will thank you for it, I promise.

Analyze Your Wins—& Losses

To heighten your intuition, it's important to think back to moments when you did—or did not—listen to it. For instance, did you have a hunch that someone you worked with was lying to you? What action did you take? Did the logical side of your brain tell you to shrug it off because you didn't have empirical evidence that they were lying, or did you trust your gut and take action in some capacity?

Perhaps you were planning to make an expensive purchase, but something inside you told you to hold off on spending that kind of money on something you didn't really need at the moment - only for you to realize you needed to spend that money on an unexpected car or home repair.

I consider these to be defining moments because they mark whether or not we trust our intuition, and they can easily serve as lessons moving forward. Here's a personal example: Recently, I was on vacation in Costa Rica. We were just heading out for the day, but I could feel my intuition compelling me to go back inside my hotel room and grab a pack of hand wipes.

I normally don't carry hand wipes in my bag, only gel, but I listened. I trusted my intuition, and I went back and retrieved the hand wipes. When my wife and I made our way to the boardwalk that morning, I noticed a woman walking in front of me who had just stepped into dog poop. She was desperately trying to clean it off with flimsy tissue.

And then it hit me. I realized the hand wipes weren't for me; they were for her. She was so grateful when I gave them to her, and I felt proud not only because I was able to help someone in need but also because I trusted my intuition and made a special effort to listen.

Create a Vision Board

I will always recommend that people on the path to success create vision boards. Why? Because they serve as daily reminders to stay dedicated to following their dreams. The more we visually acknowledge our dreams, the likelier that our subconscious mind—and our intuition—will guide us toward making our dreams a reality. Doing so provides us with a sense of child-like joy.

As kids, many of us spend time coloring or scrapbooking as a creative outlet, and there's no reason why we can't apply that same level of creativity to fulfilling our goals as adults. You can either cut out pictures from magazines and paste them onto a physical board, or you can simply copy images from Google Images and copy and paste them onto a slide in PowerPoint. You can print and laminate it or it can be used as a screensaver on your computer or phone. Either way, look at it many times a day, over and over.

Things that you can include in your personal vision board can vary. Perhaps you have a goal of achieving an executive-level position, running a marathon, or buying a new house. Simply go online and find images that connect to those goals. It may feel silly at first, but the more you do it, the more likely your intuition will latch onto them and help you achieve your goals. It's really a lot of fun!

Your sixth sense, your intuition, can be your best friend; all you have to do is listen to it. On the path to success, you may feel tempted to only listen to the logical part of your mind or the objective advice of others, and there is certainly a place for that.

But when you listen to that voice deep inside you begging you to take a certain path that the rest of your mind isn't suggesting, I highly recommend taking it seriously. You know your inner self better than anyone else, and you owe it to yourself to let your intuition guide you to the path of fulfilling your dreams because a dream-filled life is a beautiful life indeed.

To learn more, visit this website:
[https://www.sciencedaily.com/releases/2012/08/120822125028.htm]

SHANNON WHITTINGTON

About Dr. Shannon Whittington:
Shannon (she/her) is a speaker, author, consultant, and clinical nurse educator. Her area of expertise is LGBTQ+ inclusion in the workplace. Whittington has a passion for transgender health where she educates clinicians in how to care for transgender individuals after undergoing gender-affirming surgeries.

Whittington was honored to receive the Quality and Innovation Award from the Home Care Association of New York for her work with the transgender population. She was recently awarded the Notable LGBTQ+ Leaders & Executives award by Crain's New York Business, Daisy Award for Outstanding Nurses, as well as the International Association of Professionals Nurse of the Year award. Whittington is a city and state lobbyist for transgender equality.

To date, Whittington has presented virtually and in person at various organizations and conferences across the nation, delivering extremely well-received presentations. Her forthcoming books include *LGBTQ+: ABC's For Grownups* and *Kindergarten for Leaders: 9 Essential Tips For Grownup Success.*

Author's Website: *www.linkedin.com/in/ShannonWhittington*

Book Series Website: *www.The13StepsToRiches.com*

Soraiya Vasanji

JASMINE FLOWERS

What is the right choice?

How do you know something is the right choice?

Logic and reason guide the way in our decision making but something else is also communicating if you are open to hearing it. That is your sixth sense, your intuition: the self-knowing that may show up as an eye twitch, ear ringing, or nose tingle. Perhaps it's a softer inner knowing or voice speaking up. Intuition is not typically a loud burst of honking horns but rather a whispered "yes, this" or a faint red flag "not for you" resonating deep in your core.

Generally, most of us are comfortable with our five senses, and in my research, I found that, sometimes, if we have one strong sense, it can contribute to indicating when our sixth sense is chiming in. My friend's mother shared that she has a strong sense of smell, and she can always tell if she is making the right choice because she will get a whiff of flowers, especially Jasmine flowers.

It reminded her of home, particularly sitting outside and playing under her grandmother's watch near the jasmine flower bushes, where she is safe and trusts her surroundings. When the subtle notes of Jasmine tickle her nose, she knows to trust what she is doing or deciding upon. When it is not present, or when a non-floral scent kicks in, she knows it is a pass and to not go in that direction, that it is not in her best interest. How interesting! What about you? Does one of your senses alert you to your inner knowing?

Personally, my sixth sense feels magical. Time slows down for a quick moment, and a feeling of Deja vu sets in when my intuition wants me to pay a little more attention. It's usually when I am bustling out the door and have a thousand things running through my head, and this tug for my attention comes through.

I used to ignore this all the time cause I had places to be and things to do. But now I know to slow down and pay attention; there is a detail, some action, or something I am missing. Many times, it's because I have simply forgotten to grab something when heading out the door.

At other times, my sixth sense is like a clear gut reaction and a green flag saying, "Yes, this! This is RIGHT HERE! Green for GO!" Or, "Red flag, red flag, back up the bus; this is a NO-GO!" I can recall so many red flags that I ignored when my people-pleasing or perfectionist tendencies would override my sixth sense sensation.

I can recall perfectly when I first met my husband, Nadim. We were both Freshman students in Boston—he went to Harvard University, and I went to Tufts University, right next to each other. I met him in our prayer hall at the Freshman Students Welcome Night.

Even before we exchanged our names, I looked up and saw his smiling face. Well, I saw his forehead first, and time slowed, and everything felt still, so much so that it felt like I hit a pause button and was given time to take in all the details of his features.

It wasn't like when you were just glancing around a room and eye a cute guy. This was all my senses locked into this one gentleman, and I couldn't look away, nor could I scroll fast through his characteristics. Something, that inner knowing, made me truly take in this moment to tell me, "THIS IS IMPORTANT—this is your JASMINE FLOWER MOMENT!"

I knew right then that he was the one. Perhaps in that moment, I didn't fully believe that he was my soulmate and partner for life, but I knew he was the one to pay attention to, he was the one to seek out, and he was the one to turn towards. From that single day in September 2001, Nadim became my best friend, my soulmate, my partner in crime, and the one who holds my heart. (Love you, Nadim!)

Cultivating this sense is not an easy task. One way I have found to listen deeper to this voice is to not commit in the moment, to allow myself time to feel out the answer. It's shown me that my heart and gut are saying no, but something in my logic or emotions is wanting to say yes.

Afterwards, I'm at peace with my "No" and see that the universe was lining up something even better than I could have dreamed of! This happened recently with a friend who wanted to plan a mom's getaway, and my head was saying, "Yes, let's go!" but my heart was saying, "Sounds fun, but maybe we need to check in and assess the situation…."

I didn't commit or get overly zealous in the moment of the big ask, which previously I am known to do. I acknowledged the part of me that needed the break and wanted time for myself and to connect with friends.

Once I gave myself the space and time to think things through, I realized this was not the moment to take for me. My daughter was growing through some big emotions and really needed me around. My dad was having another surgery, and my parents could really use the support of their daughter. I passed on the trip and got to spend one of my best weekends with my family. We had connected time together, hearing stories, playing games, and eating yummy food. It was a bonding moment for my family where everyone was fully present and was yearning for this connection.

How did my sixth sense know? I likely didn't know what was coming, but it guided me to choose family time over an exuberant girls' trip. (By the way, the girls had fun but ended up canceling it short because they all had severe food poisoning.)

While my intuitive sense has helped me navigate some awesome times, it has also stalled my actions and saved me from something not worth doing or not worth extending myself for. I have put myself into situations where I can host awesome get-togethers and events, but people take my generosity and sincerity for granted. After cultivating my sixth sense, I know now how to uphold better boundaries to keep my special sparkle for those who appreciate and get to be showered with my gifts.

Every experience gives us signs of how to connect with our sixth sense and whether that choice was good for us or growth for us.

Here are some tips on how to connect with your intuition and free your sixth sense:

- **Solo Time!** Spend time with yourself—pure, unconditional time connecting and showing yourself the love and acknowledgment you deserve. (Does this feel hard? Can you take yourself on a date to the movies? For a walk? For dinner? What are you learning about yourself?)

- **Explore The World Around You!** When we go out to explore the world, we open ourselves to new experiences. In those moments, we tune in and heighten our senses to take in information. What do you feel or hear that is not right in front of you?

- **Get More Self Aware!** How aware are you of how you make others feel? Do you over-talk? Do you under-talk? Are you a good listener, or do you come in with your agenda first? Do you put yourself first or the collective group ahead? What are your head, heart, and body saying? What sensations are you experiencing? Are your hairs sticking up, has the temperature in your environment changed? Do you feel like you have eyes in the back of your head?

- **Ask Yourself Questions & Listen for the Answer!** I remember a fellow coach once telling me she asked herself questions for everything she did. Should she turn left or right, for example, and wait for an answer? It slowed down her life, but she truly cultivated her intuitive gift. Now, just thinking of what to do next, she knows her right course of action. It is quite spectacular!

In my personal experience, when my intuition is running at free and full capacity, my creative abilities and idea generation are limitless. This is how I know I am aligned with all my senses. This is your invitation to get curious and hone your sixth sense so you can find your Jasmine flower sign!

SORAIYA VASANJI

About Soraiya Vasanji: Soraiya is a Certified Professional Coach (CPC), Energy Leadership Index Master Practitioner (ELI-MP), and has a Master's in Business Administration (MBA) from Kellogg University. She inspires women to be present, not perfect, ditch what doesn't serve them, and create their best messy life now.

She loves sharing her wisdom on mindset, the power of language, self-love, self-worth, and leadership principles. She is the founder of the Mommy Mindset Summit series, and the Mom Mindset Reset Method coaching program. She empowers moms to move from tired, frustrated and depleted in their life to a creating the calm, happy, and emotionally-even life for them and their families—no longer swinging from "energizer bunny mom" to dead on the couch!

Soraiya is married to her soulmate, has a young daughter, and lives in Toronto, Canada. She is a foodie, a jetsetter, a doTERRA essential oil enthusiast and she loves collecting unique crafting and stationery products!

Author's Website: *www.SoraiyaVasanji.com*

Book Series Website: *www.The13StepsToRiches.com*

Stacey Ross Cohen

UNLOCK YOUR SIXTH SENSE FOR MAXIMUM POTENTIAL

"Infinite Intelligence might have a plan for you that is better than the one you came up with for yourself. The best thing to do for yourself is to learn how to listen to what it is telling you."
~ Napoleon Hill

A gut feeling, a hunch, an intuition, a guardian angel. There are many names for it, but it's a singular sensation that we can all relate to.

Napoleon Hill called it the "Sixth Sense," and he believed it necessary to tap into this sense when making decisions and seeking success and wealth. While Hill didn't believe in miracles, he did believe that the sixth sense was in many ways unexplainable—perhaps the result of a higher power or a cell structure of the brain capable of receiving thought vibrations. He also believed this sixth sense was a conduit to people's "Infinite Intelligence" and could link individuals spiritually and mentally in order to avoid danger.

This may seem extraordinary, but anyone who has had a near-accident has experienced it first-hand. The sixth sense can come to our aid quickly and inexplicably, helping us avoid a car crash or other catastrophe.

But Hill believed the sixth sense does more than save us from automobile accidents. He also thought of it as a creative tool—an instrumental through which new ideas and plans flicker into the mind. It generates not just hunches but also inspiration and eureka moments. It can help us avoid disaster but also unlock opportunity.

Mastering the Sixth Sense

Understanding and mastering the sixth sense is no easy task, according to Hill. The first step is mastering his previous twelve principles—this then unlocks access to the new sense. Mastering the sixth sense also means dispelling negative emotions like indecision, doubt, and fear. These transmit destructive vibrations and prevent the sixth sense from flourishing. Hill outlines the most common fears that hamper the sixth sense: poverty, criticism, poor health, lost love, old age, and death. He also explains that these fears are just a state of mind—and that states of mind can be changed.

There's no shortage of great leaders who succeeded in mastering their sixth sense, from Napoleon and Joan of Arc to Christ, Buddha, Confucius, and Mohammed. So, what can you do to follow in their footsteps? Hill suggests strengthening your willpower and deploying it at all times. He also recommends acknowledging your vulnerability to the six basic fears and avoiding people who promote negative influences.

Ten Ways To Develop & Strengthen Your Sixth Sense

In my own work and life, I've developed a number of strategies for honing Hill's so-called sixth sense. I'd like to share them here, as they're accessible to everyone and will likely prove helpful no matter your goals.

1. Get in Touch with Your Spiritual Side: One way to develop your sixth sense is to get in touch with your spiritual side. This can be done by meditating, attending religious services, or spending time in nature. By connecting with something larger than yourself, you can tap into a higher power that can guide you in making decisions.

2. Listen to Your Gut: Your sixth sense is often trying to communicate with you through your gut feelings. If you have a strong opinion about something, even if you don't know why, it is important to listen to it. Your gut instinct is usually right, so trust it when making decisions.

3. Pay Attention to Your Dreams: Your dreams can be a powerful source of intuition. If you're attentive to the messages you receive in your dreams, they can provide guidance and insight into both your personal life and the broader world around you. Keep a dream journal and write down any significant dreams you have so that you can interpret their meaning.

4. Remain Open to New Experiences: In order to develop your sixth sense, you must be open to new experiences. By trying new things and exposing yourself to different situations, you will be able to expand your horizons and develop a greater understanding of the world around you. Additionally, by being open to new experiences, you will also be more likely to notice the subtle cues and messages that your sixth sense is trying to send you.

5. Practice Mindfulness: Mindfulness is the practice of being present in the moment and paying attention to your thoughts, feelings, and sensations without judgment. When you are mindful, you are less likely to miss the cues your sixth sense is sending. Mindfulness has also been shown to improve mental clarity and focus, both of which are important for developing your intuition.

6. Eliminate Negative Energy: Negative energy can block your ability to connect with your sixth sense. Get rid of negative energy in your life by surrounding yourself with positive people and situations, meditating, or doing activities that make you happy. Once you have cleared out the negative energy, you will be able to better hear the messages from your sixth sense.

7. Trust Yourself: One of the most important things when it comes to developing your sixth sense is learning how to trust yourself. Listen to what your gut tells you without doubting yourself. Also, be confident in the decisions that feel right, even if others might not understand them. When you start trusting yourself, you will find it much easier to follow your sixth sense.

8. Be Patient: Rome wasn't built in a day, and neither are strong intuitive skills. Like anything else worth developing, your sixth sense requires time and patience before yielding real results. Remember: Stay open-minded during the process, and give any new techniques a try, even if they seem a bit strange at first. With a little bit of effort, eventually, you will begin to notice small changes in how you approach life—which lead to bigger changes over time.

9. Experiment in Different Ways: There are many methods of strengthening intuitive abilities, so don't feel like you need to stick to just one—especially if that one isn't working well. Some people prefer using visualization techniques, while others find success using affirmations or keeping a journal. There is no wrong way to go about this. Find what works best for *you*.

10. Seek Professional Guidance: If you're really struggling to connect with your sixth sense, then you may want to seek professional guidance, such as a psychic medium or energy healer. These individuals help clear away any blocks preventing you from accessing sixth sense abilities.

"Listen to your gut" isn't a cliche—it's sage advice. In following Napoleon Hill's guidance, you can tap into your sixth sense and start living a more productive, successful life.

STACEY ROSS COHEN

About Stacey Ross Cohen: In the world of branding, few experts possess the savvy and instinct of Stacey. An award-winning brand professional who earned her stripes on Madison Avenue and major television networks before launching her own agency, Stacey specializes in cultivating and amplifying brands.

Stacey is CEO of Co-Communications, a marketing agency headquartered in New York. She coaches businesses and individuals across a range of industries—from real estate to healthcare and education—and expertly positions their narratives in fiercely competitive markets.

A TEDx speaker, Stacey is a sought-after keynote at industry conferences and author in the realm of branding, PR, and marketing. She is a contributor at Huffington Post and Thrive Global and has been featured in *Forbes, Entrepreneur, Crain's* and a suite of other media outlets.

She holds a B.S. from Syracuse University, an MBA from Fordham University, and a certificate in Media, Technology, and Entertainment from NYU Stern School of Business.

Author's website: *www.StaceyRossCohen.com*

Book Series Website: *www.The13StepsToRiches.com*

Teresa Cundiff

CONNECTION, INSPIRATION, & INTUITION

Most people are all familiar with the words *Sixth Sense*, but I think that if you ask five people what they think it is, you'll get five different answers. In 1972, there was a television show starring Gary Collins called *The Sixth Sense*. In 1999, there was a movie starring Bruce Willis and Haley Joel Osment called *The Sixth Sense* with the famous line, "I see dead people." Both of these are intriguing, and we watch because we are curious about supernatural things. Some people are described as having a sixth sense because they seem to know things before they happen. But what is it really?

My own experience with having a sixth sense is that streetlights turn off when I pass underneath them. This has been happening to me since I was in college and still happens today. It's a crazy kind of thing, and I can only chalk it up to some type of supernatural thing I have. It happens regardless of the vehicle I'm driving or my geographic location, or if other people are in the car with me. My college boyfriend called it, "Freaky!" I can do nothing to control it, and it doesn't happen with every streetlight. I just know that when the streetlight goes out, it's me!

Dictionary.com defines the sixth sense as a power of perception beyond the five senses: intuition. We should all be familiar with the phrase, "Woman's intuition." It's that sixth sense that makes itself known when a woman makes a call based on a feeling of knowing what will happen, "Call it woman's intuition," people will say. It's also interesting to note that there is no common phrase called "Man's intuition" that has ever been used. I wonder why!

Sometimes, we have that sixth sense with people we are connected to. When my oldest son, John, was in high school, we had a very strong connection with our hearts and our minds. As soon as I would reach out to ask him where he was, he would be turning into the neighborhood or driveway. This happened very frequently. And it wasn't because I was watching the time and knew when he left from somewhere. It's more like I could feel him coming closer to me in a sixth sense kind of way. No communication was necessary.

My younger son, Jake, and I are connected through all the things we have in common. He and I both worked together at our local professional theater for a number of years. We both love to visit New York City and take in as many shows as we possibly can while we are there. We think alike and feel alike in so many ways. A mom has a connection to her children that moms understand.

Then comes inspiration. I can think of the things that have inspired me or moved me in some way over the course of my life, and to me, that is a feeling of a sixth sense. We lived in Ft. Leavenworth, Kansas, from 2001-2002 while my husband attended Command and General Staff College. It was a very short year of school for him, John, and Jake. Ft. Leavenworth, the post, is positioned right behind the Leavenworth Federal Penitentiary. Now, you may have seen correctional institutions in your travels, but I promise you that you will never forget laying your eyes on a federal penitentiary! It is one of the most sobering sights I have ever seen, and it does serve as inspiration as a cautionary tale when raising my sons.

Imagine driving by it for the first time. The front of the giant structure looks like the Capital Building in Washington, DC, but twice the number of columns on both sides of the center entrance that has a dome over the top of it. It was called Big Top, while the US Army Disciplinary Barracks was called Little Top when we lived there. The Army has since built a new prison, which was under construction when we lived there. It was fascinating to me to think about all the men who were housed inside.

Then, as the road it sits on continues west, and we make our right turn to go in the second gate of the post, there is a massive field where buffalo are grazing and a smaller facility with an outdoor track. But the incredible sight to behold is the length of the prison wall facing us. The outside perimeter is 3030 ft, and the campus takes up 22.8 acres. It was just a long, white wall that is higher than you might expect—no windows at all. The prisoners would only ever see what was enclosed and nothing more. No touch of the outside world whatsoever.

No matter how many times we drove past it, entering and exiting the post, the sight of the federal pen gave me pause. My boys were six and nine at the time, and I steeled in my heart that they would never be in such a situation as to land themselves in a place like that. It's a punishment for sure, and no one would ever want to go there twice, having experienced it once. So, the inspiration I took from our few months at Ft. Leavenworth was that I would be involved and present in my son's lives and lift them up prayerfully to God for protection to never go to such a place.

Another thing that is inspiring is the Statue of Liberty. She is beautiful and majestic and another sight to behold. The history contained on Ellis Island is bountiful. Every time we visit New York City and ride the ferry out to see her, it gives me a supernatural feeling. Another statue that will stop you dead in your tracks is the Lincoln Memorial! It is magnificent! Lincoln sits there and is so big that I think my jaw went slack upon seeing it the first time. I was born on Lincoln's birthday, so I have an affection for him as more than the president who saved our Union. It is very fitting for him to have such a monument.

When it comes to intuition, I feel like this property of the sixth sense is when we know something is right or something is wrong from the jump. This is also discernment. I personally don't feel like I have a strong intuition about anything other than my children. But sometimes, I can feel a thing in my gut that informs my decision-making. Another phrase here is "gut instinct." I supposed that's the phrase for men that is juxtaposed to women's intuition. Something to think about.

Can you think of a time when you went against your intuition or instinct and things turned out less than favorably? I don't want to say it turned out badly because when things don't turn out the way we planned or foresaw, it's not always bad—just different. When that happens, we say to ourselves, "Should have trusted my intuition!" or "Should have gone with my gut!" From there, we learn the lesson, apply it, and tune in more closely to what we feel in our bodies when faced with varying circumstances.

Napoleon Hill describes the Sixth Sense as that portion of the subconscious mind that has been referred to as the creative imagination. It has also been referred to as the "receiving set" through which ideas, plans, and thoughts flash into the mind. The "flashes" are sometimes called "hunches" or "inspirations." He says the sixth sense is a mixture of both the spiritual and the mental. He goes on to tell of his imaginary counsel of men who convene around a table in his mind. It's very fascinating. He also says that mastery of the first twelve principles of *Think and Grow Rich* is necessary to develop the sixth sense. Armed with this information, I feel like I need to go back to the beginning and start reading his book anew.

I have loved being on this journey as you have read *The 13 Steps to Riches.* My being part of this collaboration effort with my fellow authors has enriched my life greatly. I had no sixth sense premonition that these thirteen books would be so wildly successful! I am so grateful to Eric Swanson and Jon Kovach, Jr. for this incredible opportunity to be part of something so much larger than myself! Thank you for thinking enough of me to invite me to be part of this collaboration effort! The journey has been so worthwhile and meaningful! I am forever changed by this writing experience and knowing the other thirty-two authors in these books!

I hope as you read this final book in the set that you have been informed, moved, and inspired to do great things! My contact info is listed here. Please reach out if I may be of service to you! Thank you for reading our books!

TERESA CUNDIFF

About Teresa Cundiff: Cundiff is a freelance proofreader with the tagline, "I know where the commas go!" Teresa makes her clients work shine with her knowledge of grammar, punctuation, and sentence structure.

Teresa is a ten-time International Bestselling Contributing Author of *1 Habit for Entrepreneurial Success, 1 Habit to Thrive in a Post-COVID World*, and four *The Art of Connection* books. All of which are placed in the Library of Congress. Other titles include, *The Book I read* and *People Who Get $h!t Done*. She is a twelve-time Bestselling Contributing Author to *The 13 Steps to Riches* Series.

Teresa is a Master Mentor and Divisional Director Candidate with GIVERS University.

Author's Website: *www.linktr.ee.com/TeresaCundiff*

Book Series Website: *www.The13StepsToRiches.com*

Vera Thomas

LEAD ME—GUIDE ME

Lamp to My Feet

Light to my path
Holy Spirit—a sixth sense
Is what I seek
Wisdom, insight
From a higher power
Gives me joy
Brings me peace.
Every day and every hour.

In *Think and Grow Rich*, this quote amply depicts the source:

"Through the aid of the sixth sense, you will be warned of impending dangers in time to avoid them and notified of opportunities in time to embrace them.

There comes to your aid, and to do your bidding, with the development of the sixth sense, a "guardian angel" who will open to you at all times the door to the Temple of Wisdom."

This depiction sounds much like my experience with the Holy Spirit. Some refer to the sixth sense as intuition, insight, clairvoyance, extrasensory perception (ESP), foresight, or premonition. Second sight, telepathy, and gut feeling may also be referred to as the sixth sense. These terms collectively illustrate the concept of "the sixth sense" as not merely a supernatural ability but also an inherent human capacity for deeper understanding and awareness that transcends ordinary perception. It is believed we all have this to varying degrees that can be nurtured and embraced.

I would like to add another reference, the Holy Spirit. I want to dive into the differences, similarities, and experiences. My comparison is not to minimize either. It is to express how both can be of benefit to one's purpose, passion, and vision.

Napoleon Hill indicated one must master the other principles to fully experience a sixth sense. The development of one's sixth sense is congruent with the development of being in tune with the Holy Spirit. To activate the sixth sense, one does not necessarily need to be connected to a form of spirituality. However, connecting to the higher self, spirit, and universe can enhance the effects of the sixth sense.

The concept of a "sixth sense" and the Holy Spirit are often discussed in spiritual contexts, but they have distinct differences and similarities. Let us compare these two concepts:

Sixth Sense:

- Often described as an intuitive ability or extrasensory perception
- Typically viewed as a natural or innate human capability
- Not necessarily tied to any specific religious belief

Holy Spirit:

- Third person of the Christian Trinity
- Divine in nature, part of the Godhead
- Specifically tied to Christian theology and belief

In understanding the sixth sense, these are some things to consider:

1. **Natural Human Ability:** Many view the sixth sense as an innate human capability that everyone possesses to some degree rather than something exclusively tied to spirituality or religion. The ability to perceive, feel the atmosphere, and sense things are examples of innate abilities.

2. **Intuitive Intelligence:** The sixth sense is often described as intuitive intelligence or an internal energetic awareness centered in the heart, gut, and possibly skin.

3. **Meditation & Mindfulness:** Regular meditation or mindfulness practices can help develop and clarify sixth sense perceptions by stilling the thinking mind and allowing one to tune into subtler impressions. Concentration on breathing can begin the process of mindfulness.

4. **Connection to Higher Self:** Some believe that connecting with one's "higher self" or inner spirit can enhance intuitive abilities. This can be achieved through various spiritual practices not necessarily tied to organized religion. As a believer, that higher self that lives within is the Holy Spirit.

5. **Energy Awareness:** Developing sensitivity to subtle energies and vibrations is often associated with sixth sense abilities. This can be cultivated through various spiritual or energy-based practices.

6. **Daily Practice:** Regularly taking time to quiet the mind, listening to one's inner guidance, and paying attention to subtle impressions can help develop sixth sense abilities, regardless of specific spiritual beliefs.

7. **Openness & Trust:** Being open to the possibility of extrasensory perception and learning to trust one's intuitive impressions is important for developing these abilities.

I acknowledge there are distinct differences; however, the demonstration of both may be similar. Both are more developed through meditation, prayer, and mindfulness.

Both concepts relate to perception beyond the five physical senses. The Holy Spirit is a distinctly Christian concept with divine attributes, whereas the sixth sense is a more general term often associated with natural intuition or extrasensory perception. Christians are encouraged to rely on the Holy Spirit for guidance rather than any form of sixth sense or extrasensory perception.

Similarities:

1. **Enhanced Perception:** Both are associated with an ability to perceive things beyond normal human senses. The sixth sense is often described as intuition or extrasensory perception, while the Holy Spirit is said to provide spiritual discernment and guidance.

2. **Source of Insight:** Both are viewed as sources of knowledge or understanding that goes beyond ordinary cognition. The sixth sense is seen as providing intuitive insights, while the Holy Spirit offers spiritual wisdom and understanding.

3. **Guidance:** Both concepts are associated with providing direction or guidance. The sixth sense is often described as an inner guide, while the Holy Spirit is seen as a divine guide for believers.

Key Differences:

1. **Origin & Nature:** The sixth sense is generally viewed as a natural human ability, while the Holy Spirit is understood in Christianity as a divine person, part of the Trinity living within us.

2. **Accessibility:** The sixth sense is often considered a latent ability in all humans, while the Holy Spirit is believed to indwell only Christian believers. There is a spirit that indwells inside of all of us (a topic for future discussion).

3. **Purpose:** The sixth sense is usually associated with general intuition or paranormal abilities, while the Holy Spirit has specific spiritual purposes in Christian theology, such as convicting of sin, empowering for ministry, guiding into truth, and a daily walk.

4. **Reliability:** The sixth sense is subjective and not universally reliable, while Christians believe the Holy Spirit to be infallible and always truthful.

While I know we all have a sixth sense that is developed or developing, I know and trust the Holy Spirit without doubt as infallible and always truthful. This is not intended to negate any faith or belief in the sixth sense. I can only share my experiences.

As a reminder, previously, I quoted Hill:

> *"...you will be warned of impending dangers in time to avoid them and notified of opportunities in time to embrace them.*
>
> *There comes to your aid, and to do your bidding, with the development of the sixth sense, a "guardian angel" who will open to you at all times the door to the Temple of Wisdom."*

This has been the Holy Spirit for me. There is not enough time or space in this chapter to enumerate them all.

I have learned that the Holy Spirit speaks in various ways: dreams, a still small voice, angels, through others, or directly through His Word. I have experienced all the ways. I have also learned that obedience is better than sacrifice. When the Spirit speaks, I need to listen. When I do not, it is clearly evident. There are consequences either way.

The day I got married, I distinctly heard, "You should not be doing this!" I had ten bridesmaids, a church full of people, and we had created and recorded all the songs for our wedding, "I should not be doing this?" I did it anyway. Three years of physical, mental, and emotional abuse. My blessing, my son.

I believe, as scripture says, "Thy Word is a lamp unto my feet, and a light unto my path" (Psalm 119:105 KJV) and, "If any of you lack wisdom, let him ask of God, that giveth to all men liberally, and upbraided not; and it shall be given him" (James 1:5).

The day I was leaving Los Angeles, I was offered a job. They begged me to stay. I told them I would call them back. I got my Bible and said, "Show me through your Word what I am to do." I opened the Bible, and the first thing I saw was, "Go home to thy friends and tell them what great things the Lord has done for you and how he has had compassion on you."

I went home. My plan was to be there for no more than three years and move on. Every time I had intentions of leaving (at least five occasions), I would ask, and each time I heard Spirit say, "Stay where you are!" Against my desire, I was told for twenty-five years, "Stay where you are!" I would not have acquired the education or myriads of opportunities to develop programs for youth and adults, fathers, families, or the ICF coach I am today had I left Ohio each time I wanted to.

Spiritual Significance: The Holy Spirit has a central role in Christian faith and practice, while the sixth sense is a more general concept not tied to any specific religious belief.

References:

The Sixth Sense: Barre Center for Buddhist Studies
www.Buddhistinquiry.org/article/The-Sixth-Sense
Thesaurus/Dictionary
www.Thesaurus.yourdictionary.com/Sixth-Sense
Your Sixth Sense
www.EdNewton.com/Blog/2022/06/29/Your-Sixth-Sense
Your Sixth Sense and the Holy Spirit
www.EastBrook.org/Your-Sixth-Sense-the-Holy-Spirit
Touching Lives
www.TouchingLives.org/Devotionals/Sixth-Sense

VERA THOMAS

About Vera Thomas: Vera Thomas is an ICF Certified Life Coach, International Speaker, Trainer, Mediator, Poet, 25x Bestselling Author, and Producer of a bi-weekly podcast/radio show, "The Vera Thomas Show." Her show is on Tuesdays and Thursdays at 7 pm EST.

Vera has worked with companies, organizations, schools, churches, and non-profits developing, designing, and delivering training and leadership programs. As a Certified Coach, Vera works with families, children and individuals.

As an international speaker she has spoken to groups of all ages and stages all over the world. Vera is available for companies who want to transform their teams or families who want to transform their lives.

Author's Website: *www.bit.ly/VeraThomas*

Book Series Website: *www.The13StepsToRiches.com*

Yuri Choi

CREATIVE IMAGINATION

When was the last time you just *knew* something was going to happen?

Not a logical knowing, but a deep, quiet truth bubbling up from somewhere beyond your mind—an intuition that felt like home, even if you couldn't explain it.

Most of us have been taught to look to the past to predict our future, to stay in the safety of what we know, and to guard ourselves against the unknown. And though, what if the future isn't something we stumble into or calculate but something we genuinely have the power to create? What if all it takes is a little courage to dream, a little trust in our own knowing, and a wild willingness to believe?

Eight years ago, I was in a corporate job that felt like a box I couldn't escape. I told myself there was no other path. I'd built walls of "shoulds" around me, keeping my dreams of helping people as a coach and writing books to become an author at more than arm's length. Still, I couldn't silence the whisper of a life that was meant to feel fuller, more alive.

That's when I discovered *The Secret*, a documentary about the Laws of Attraction. I began watching it daily that first year, not because I believed right away, but because I needed to feel that hope was real. Each viewing cracked my walls a little more, like light pouring through a once-closed window. I started to imagine a world where I could be free, where doors opened simply because I believed they could.

As I watched, I found myself wondering about the people in the film. I'd envision myself talking with them, sharing ideas as if they were close friends. I started to feel what it might be like to meet John Assaraf, who spoke so beautifully about the power of vision boards. I'd think about Marie Diamond, who shared how our environments—the paintings, the spaces around us—could shape what we bring into our lives. And in those quiet moments, I began to ask myself: *What would it feel like to create something with people like them?*

Back then, they were only figures on a screen. But now, looking back, I see that these little dreams weren't just fantasies. They were something deeper. Napoleon Hill calls it "creative imagination"—a kind of magical knowing that pulls us toward what's meant to be. I didn't realize it at the time, but I was already weaving the first threads of a life that hadn't yet unfolded.

And here we are. This very book series you're holding is a collaboration with John Assaraf and Marie Diamond. The people I once only dreamed of working with are now co-creators on this journey. That dream I had, sitting alone and watching *The Secret*, has become real.

But that's just one story. The more I leaned into that magic, the more I saw impossible things come to life. Each time, I felt more certain that dreams are not distant fantasies. They are blueprints we carry in our souls, waiting to be built.

In 2018, I picked up *Think and Grow Rich* for the first time. It was like finding a map of a world I'd always sensed but couldn't see. It was strange at first, to allow myself to dream so boldly. I felt a little shy, a little afraid of disappointment. But I couldn't deny how alive it made me feel. I began to ask myself, "What would it look like to dream wildly, without limits?"

One of my deepest passions has always been to end the stigma around mental health and well-being. It felt like a calling, something bigger than me. I remember writing in my vision sheet, "I am teaching millions to meditate and showing them the power of infinite possibility." It felt surreal to write those words, like looking out over the edge of a cliff. But each day I read them, and each day, a little more doubt dissolved, replaced by something new—something that felt like faith.

Then, one day, a message popped up on my Facebook page. It was from a man who had seen one of my videos. At the time, I had only a small YouTube channel with a few hundred followers. The message was simple. He liked my energy and wanted to know if I could coach him. Nothing out of the ordinary, it seemed, but I felt something—a pull, like a soft hum in the background, a note that felt familiar.

As we spoke, I discovered who he was. This was the founder and CEO of Psych2Go, the largest mental health YouTube channel in the world, with 2.3 million subscribers at the time. He became my coaching client, and together, we dove into the power of visualization, mindset, and manifesting. He began to dream bigger, too, and as he did, his channel grew to reach millions more.

A few years into our work, he came to me with a question. "I love everything you're teaching me," he said. "Would you be open to doing a live workshop with my audience? Maybe we could meditate together?"

And just like that, I found myself speaking to people from all over the world, sharing the very tools I'd once used to lift myself from doubt to hope. The vision I'd once written in the quiet of my room had become my reality.

Sometimes, I wonder: Did I manifest this, or was it always meant to be, waiting for me to find it?

Think and Grow Rich teaches us that when we're clear about our purpose, when we believe in ourselves and nurture unwavering faith, our creative imagination steps in to guide us. Napoleon Hill calls this intuition our "sixth sense"—a knowing that doesn't need proof.

When we choose to dream and trust in our vision, this knowing becomes like a compass, pulling us forward. It's as if the universe, like a master artist, is moving in harmony with our desires, aligning us with the very path we came here to walk.

Just as there is a force that governs the stars and moves the tides, I believe there is a force that lives within each of us, a spark that calls us to grow, to create, to step into who we truly are. And the more we listen, the louder that voice becomes. The more we trust, the more magic finds its way to us.

So, I'll leave you with this: What are the stories in your life where you've felt that spark of intuition, where you sensed the power of your dreams pulling you toward something greater?

And if you let yourself fully trust in that power, if you let yourself believe without hesitation—what could become possible for you?

YURI CHOI

About Yuri Choi: Yuri is Founder of Yuri Choi Coaching. Choi is a performance coach for entrepreneurs and high achievers. She helps them create and stay in a powerful, abundant, unstoppable mindset to achieve their goals by helping them gain clarity and understanding, leverage their emotional states, and create empowering habits and language patterns.

She is a speaker, writer, creator, connector, YouTuber, and the author of Creating Your Own Happiness. Choi is passionate about spreading the messages about meditation, power of intention, and creating a powerful mindset to live a fulfilling life. She is also a Habitude Warrior Conference Speaker and emcee, and she is also a designated guest coach for Psych2Go, the largest online mental health magazine and YouTube Channel. Her mission in the world is to inspire people to live leading with L.O.V.E. (which stands for: laughter, oneness, vulnerability, and ease) and to ignite people's souls to live in a world of infinite creative possibilities and abundance.

Author's Website: *www.YuriChoiCoaching.com*

Book Series Website: *www.The13StepsToRiches.com*

GRAB YOUR COPY OF AN OFFICIAL PUBLICATION
WITH THE ORIGINAL UNEDITED TEXT FROM 1937
BY THE NAPOLEON HILL FOUNDATION!

THE NAPOLEON HILL FOUNDATION
WWW.NAPHILL.ORG

Habitude Warrior Mastermind

Join a team of
AWESOME
Entrepreneurs, Coaches, Business Owners, and Leaders to support you in your journey of success!

Be one of my personal guests for a session!
www.MastermindGuestPass.com

HABITUDE WARRIOR & INTEGRITY PUBLISHING EDITORIAL TEAM

Habitude Warrior International and Integrity Publishing take great pride in our editorial team, who puts their sweat, tears, and heart into each and every project and national bestseller! Thank you, team!

JON KOVACH JR.
Team Manager

PAT MINTON
VP of Operations

JILLIAN KOVACH
Editorial Manager

Jon Kovach Jr. strives to assist every author and every team member in the process of self-development for ultimate success.

Pat Minton has been with the Habitude Warrior International team for over 20 years, getting her start with Brian Tracy & Erik Swanson.

Jillian is a vital team member of Habitude Warrior & Integrity Publishing, bringing her expertise managing our Editorial Department.

FATIMA HURD
Editorial Team & Photographer

LAUREN COBB
Editorial Team Member

Fatima is our Professional Photographer for Habitude Warrior as well as one of our members on the Proofing Department team.

Lauren Cobb is part of our Proofing Department for Habitude Warrior & Integrity Publishing as well as one of our authors.

To inquire about joining our team please send us an email to Team@HabitudeWarrior.com

www.ingramcontent.com/pod-product-compliance
Lightning Source LLC
Chambersburg PA
CBHW051300120626
46547CB00015B/2022